CELEBRATING PORTSMOUTH

JOHN SADDEN

AMBERLEY

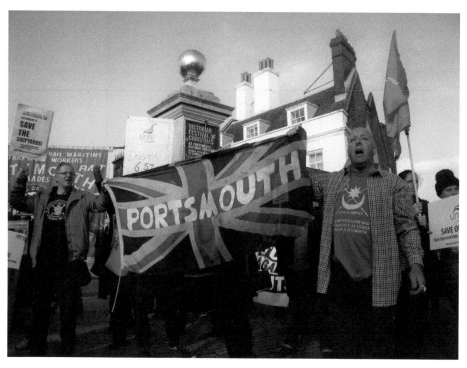

Patriotic demonstrators fight against job losses at the main gate of Portsmouth Dockyard, 2014.

First published 2022

Amberley Publishing, The Hill, Stroud
Gloucestershire GL5 4EP

www.amberley-books.com

British Library Cataloguing in Publication Data.
A catalogue record for this book is available from the British Library.

ISBN 978 1 3981 0418 1 (print)
ISBN 978 1 3981 0419 8 (ebook)

Typesetting by SJmagic DESIGN SERVICES, India.
Printed in Great Britain.

Contents

Introduction   4

1 God Save the Queen   5

2 The Guildhall   8

3 The News   16

4 Celebrating Dickens   20

5 Celebrating Portsmouth's Literary Influence   25

6 Chuck Us a Penny, Mister!   29

7 Down the Market   32

8 The Canoe Lake   39

9 Celebrating the Life of Spice   45

10 The Camber   50

11 Give 'er a Cheer, Boys!   53

12 Ships Ahoy!   57

13 Celebrating Education for All   59

14 The Common for the People   64

15 Walking on Water   75

16 Play up Pompey!   81

17 Spinnaker Tower   83

18 Cathedral City   85

19 Celebrating the Spirit of Portsmouth   88

Selected References   96

Introduction

There is plenty to celebrate about the history of Portsmouth and Southsea. Many books and websites have done so, often concentrating on the area's rich maritime history and chronological historical development, but there are some aspects, less celebrated but worthy of attention, which have contributed to the city's unique spirit, shape and character. It is a very select few of these that this book largely focuses on.

What shapes and makes the city, apart from its geography and natural resources, is its people. Over the years, through individual effort, entrepreneurship, innovation, bloody-mindedness and collective action, they have made their city a proud one, rich in history and achievement.

The city's inspirational motto – 'Heaven's light our guide' – is comparatively recent, having been formally registered and adopted in 1929. By any measure, not every local elected councillor or Member of Parliament has been on the side of the angels, but many have been motivated by a love of the city and its people and have done their best to represent them and make the city a better place. But, inevitably, the corollary of 'Heaven's light our guide' – that the road to hell is paved with good intentions – sometimes kicks in. This book is about celebration, reflecting an enduring love of Portsmouth while also recognising that true love means embracing contradictions and flaws.

Acknowledgments and Picture Credits

With thanks to Jo Godfree for her suggestions, to the artist Karl Rudziak for kind permission to reproduce Sandra's portrait (p95 bottom), photographer Tony Hicks for his drone photography (p84 bottom) and Sarah Quail for the photo on p88(from Suffering & Suffrage in Portsmouth).

Author photography: 2, 7, 18, 19, 24, 26, 34, 37B, 38TB, 74, 82MB, 83, 84T, 87B, 93B, 94TMB, 95TB. W.Burbage: 6R, 14, 15, 48T, 52B, 58TB, 61B, 82T, 87T, 93T. Rock Bros: Cover photo, 6R, 9B, 29, 41T, 69B, 71B, 76T, 77B, 80B, 86. N.Barber:28B, 50B, 51TMB, 52TM. Portsmouth Grammar School:45, 58, 65. Gates (Snape) Portsmouth in the Past (1926):9T, 22, 47T, 62.SB Henderson:31.Gates: Records of Corporation:33. Graphic:30, 54T, 63.HW Mills: 55T, 72T, 78T.Cribb: 56T, 56BL. Southsea Guides (1930s):43B, 78B.D.Ltd.:12.LS & Co.:20.W.Strang from Plain Tales from the Hills (1904):25.C.Beresford (WikiCommons):27T.FGO Stuart:27B.G.Bain (WikiCommons)28T.British Mirror Series:41B.JW Welch:43T.Lovett (Shadow Tales of Portsmouth Cathedral):46B.E.Ward:47B.Coal Exchange:48B.Still & West:49B. Queen Victoria's Jubilee Book:54B.Cozens:55B.M&Co:57.Calcutt & Beavis:71T.Woolstone Bros:72B.G.Kinch:73.Pictorial Printing & Publishing Co:76B.Hampshire Pageant (Telegraph)16, 81. Publisher not known/author's collection:11, 16, 62, 69T, 85.

1

God Save the Queen

Dreadful and wonderful things happened in Queen Victoria's reign and in her name. As Britain's premier naval port and a garrison town, Portsmouth, and its people, played a key role in maintaining and extending the British Empire. In recent years there has been discussion about the appropriateness of some public statues and monuments prompted by the Black Lives Matter movement, and it will be interesting to see how this develops in the years to come. In 1937, the *Portsmouth Evening News* mentioned a novel called *The White Flamingo* in which 'the authoress related the adventures of a society formed for the purpose of destroying England's ugly monuments'. The society made a raid on Portsmouth, taking away, in the dead of night, the statue of Queen Victoria in the Guildhall Square.

There is no dispute that the real Queen was, by the standards of the time, or any time, plain. The word is a constant in many physical descriptions of her, along with 'short' and 'dumpy'. The challenge for sculptor Alfred Drury, then, was immense when he was commissioned to create a bronze statue to be situated prominently in the Town Hall Square.

Following the Queen's death in 1901, fundraising was launched to properly honour and celebrate her long reign. An initial proposal to erect a sanatorium for consumptives on the slopes of Portsdown Hill was adopted, but fundraising fell well short. Instead, the Mayor, Sir William Dupree, launched the statue fund with a donation of by far the largest sum – £200 – and many local brewers, whose fortunes were substantially made refreshing officers and men of Her Majesty's Army and Navy, gave modest sums. Portsmouth Police Band put on a concert and other events were held in the Town Hall to boost the fund. Poor children of the local Board Schools staged exhibitions of drill, raising over £50, while the loyal, working-class inhabitants of Sydenham Terrace scraped together eight shillings and sixpence.

It had been hoped that a member of the royal family would do the honours but, on 17 July 1903, Alfred Drury's bronze statue was unveiled by the Mayoress in a ceremony attended by an estimated 16,000 people. It stood in the Town Hall Square opposite Park Road. The local press reported that 'from the railway bridge to the Theatre Royal the people stood in a solid mass'. The crowd included sailors of a visiting American squadron, alongside local servicemen and Portsmouth people of all classes, though those of higher status – what were described as 'a large number of favoured ones' – were able to view the ceremony from the Town Hall steps 'in most comfortable fashion'.

After the cord had been pulled and the covering removed, it was agreed that Drury had produced 'an imposing piece of work' that truly represented 'her late majesty in flowing robes, stately and matronly'. At 11 feet tall she was no longer short, but the sculptor had maintained her proportions and she was identifiably who she was supposed to be. The crowd cheered and went off to add to the brewers' profits.

By 1937, the Town Square had completely changed in character with the growing popularity of the motor car and the need to widen roads. The old Queen was no longer surrounded by trees and benches where people could sit and quietly reflect on her reign between the chimes from the Town Hall. She was now surrounded by noisy, dirty traffic and prostitutes plying their trade, the square being a notorious pick-up point. It was recommended that the statue be moved to a better site 'in more delightful surroundings', but she stayed put

Below left: The Town Hall square and statue of Queen Victoria.

Below right: The Queen in 1972 (with the Gas Board offices – now Wetherspoon's – in the background).

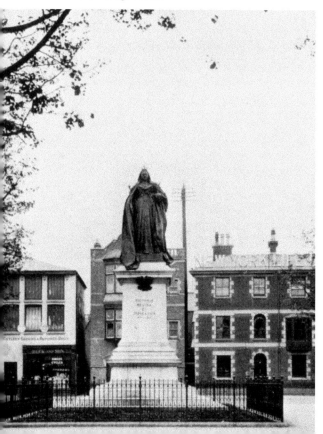 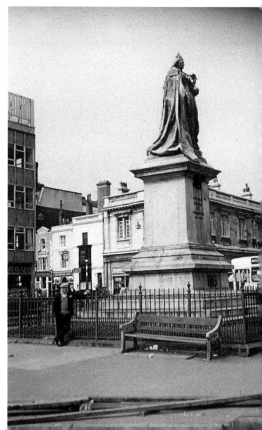

and witnessed what was now called the Guildhall reduced to a shell by the Luftwaffe.

By the 1950s she was caged in 'unsightly railings' for her own protection and needed a good clean, her majestic robes now resembling 'a sailor's old oilskin'. Others described the statue simply as 'a monstrosity'. Pevsner described her as 'aged and plump'. One suggestion in the local press was that she be painted, another that she be used as a 'spire' on the re-emergent Guildhall, which if you look at the photo on the front of this book looks strangely possible. Mercifully, Her bronze Majesty was spared these indignities.

Post-war planning of the bustling city centre was dominated by the needs of motorists, with the number of registered vehicles having more than doubled in a decade. In the 1970s, a ring road was built and the Guildhall Square redeveloped and pedestrianised. The old Queen – who by now was listed as of Special Architectural or Historic Interest – was restored and re-sited in a more prominent central position facing the Guildhall, enabling passers-by to fully appreciate the statue at their leisure, at the same time as enjoying the changing reflections of the Guildhall in the black mirrored windows of the civic offices behind her.

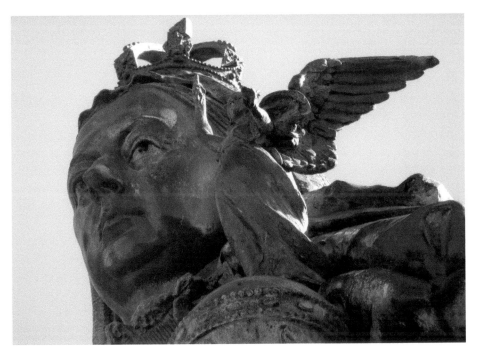

Under the Queen's gaze.

The Guildhall

The first mayor of Portsmouth, Thomas Carpenter, was elected in 1531 during the reign of Henry VIII. Carpenter was a wealthy man and built the first town hall, prominently and at his own expense, in the middle of the High Street. In the preceding centuries there was likely to have been a common hall or moot-hall where community matters were discussed and settled, though it was also the practice in some villages and settlements for the nave or vestry of the local church to be used. Carpenter's town hall was probably a timber structure. It had a court or council chamber and other rooms including one occupied by the senior Sergeant at Mace. A long range of shambles, as well as stalls for a fish market, were aligned in the street, running from the junction with what is now Pembroke Road. From 1693, the mayor received the rents and was expected to keep the buildings in good repair.

After two centuries the building had become 'ruinous' and some of the town's business was conducted in 'the Great Room at Goddes House' (Government House on Governor's Green). In 1739 the wooden hall was dismantled and a new stone building erected with ornamental features including stucco ceilings and 'vases set over the pilasters of the portico'. Described as ugly, it was 'the rendezvous, by night under the arches, of the idle and profligate', a description which is believed not to refer to the mayor and burgesses awaiting entrance to the chamber. There is a report that, during a mayor's banquet, 'a mischievous wag' released a lot of sparrows, extinguishing all the candles and throwing the distinguished party into darkness. By 1795, the Council Chamber was considered too small and it was rebuilt on Corinthian pillars with steps leading up to it, beneath which was a marketplace.

The nineteenth century brought with it a rapid growth in population and traffic and the Town Hall had become a serious obstruction, the two narrow thoroughfares each side creating a bottleneck. The butchers' shambles was removed to help ease the problem but to little effect, and so it was decided to relocate and build a new town hall. Adjacent land was bought on the south side of the High Street, neighbouring Portsmouth's reputedly oldest surviving pub, The Dolphin. While it was under construction, meetings were held in the jail in Penny

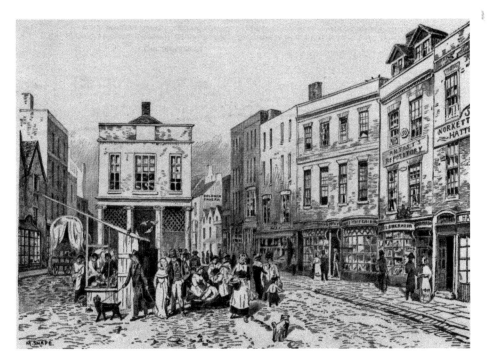

Above: The Town Hall, erected
in the High Street in 1739.

Right: The Guildhall and
marketplace, opened in 1838.

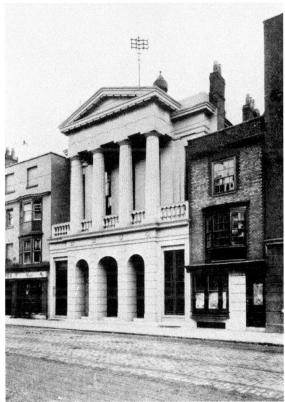

Street (which stood on the site of what is now the Portsmouth Grammar School theatre and dining hall).

The new 'Guildhall and Market-House' boasted a grand façade and was built along with a police station near the corner of Pembroke Road at a total cost of £4,500. The opening was timed to coincide with Queen Victoria's Coronation day in 1838 – at 5 o'clock in the morning. The local press reported that a huge number of the local population turned out to witness the ceremonial opening but that, in the event, a humble town crier barked the honours. It was reported that neither the mayor or any member of the building committee was present to 'say something' and that the occasion 'passed over rather flatly'. This building was, in turn, superseded and in 1890 was converted to serve as the town museum until it was bombed in the Second World War.

The foundation stone for the next Town Hall was laid in 1884 following the purchase of a house and 3.5 acres of land in Landport, a central location which recognised that there was more to the town than Old Portsmouth. The residence had been occupied by the commanding officer of the local artillery, but many years earlier it had belonged to a brewer, Alderman Thomas Ridge. In 1710 there had been a Parliamentary investigation into the conduct of Ridge, Queen's cooper, who was one of the main contractors supplying beer and casks to the navy at Portsmouth, who also sat as the MP for Poole. He was exposed as having defrauded the Crown of £19,000 and was expelled from the House of Commons. But, then as now, being routinely dishonest or corrupt was no hindrance to political advancement and he was re-elected as an alderman in 1711 and returned again to Parliament in 1722.

When the foundations for the new town hall were being dug out, a decapitated skeleton with the skull lying beside it was found alongside some other human bones. As the small roots of ancient trees were found entwined around them it was concluded that they had been buried many years earlier. The new Town Hall cost £137,098 and two labourers' lives, and took four years to build, at a time when there was little or no official or employer concern for workers' safety.

The design that had been chosen was almost a replica of the town hall at Bolton but on a grander scale. That, in turn, had clearly been inspired by the town hall at Leeds which had been built in the 1850s, so Portsmouth's new Town Hall was already old-fashioned when it was completed in 1890. Heavy Italianate Classical in style, built of white Portland stone, it was celebrated for bringing a touch of class to a grubby dockyard town.

All municipal departments were accommodated under one roof, along with a hall with seating for 2,000 people and a public library. Its clock was 'of exceptional size being second to that at Westminster', and the hours and quarter-hours were sounded on five bells that weighed over 6 tons. The quarter-hours rang out the 'Pompey Chimes' which were to become known the world over. The total height was 206 feet, making it 'one of the most imposing structures in the town'. Two lions guarded a broad flight of granite steps leading to a grand entrance that was only to be used on state occasions.

The tympanum – the group of sculptures inside the pediment above the portico that forms part of the main entrance to the Town Hall – was commissioned from the sculptor Henry Thomas Garretson of Chelsea, and celebrated trade and Empire. Britannia dominates in the centre, surrounded by allegorical figures of

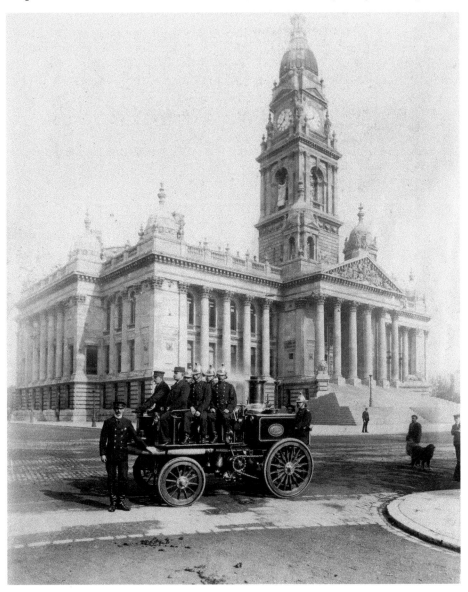

Civic assets – a new fire engine showcased outside the fire station and Town Hall in the early 1900s.

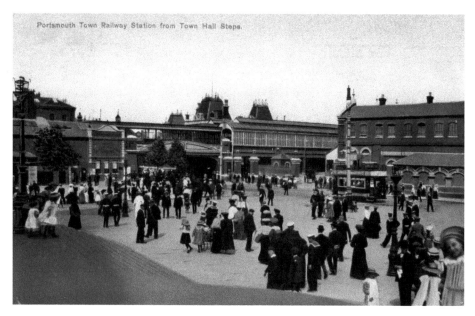

Portsmouth Town Railway Station from Town Hall Steps.

View from the Town Hall steps, *c.* 1910.

the continents, whose states of undress indicated perceived levels of civilisation, along with an Indian elephant, a camel and a bison and other figures, crowned by Neptune in his chariot.

The design was described by Pevsner as 'one of the grander gestures of late-Victorian municipal pride', suggesting that there is nothing else of the period south of the Midlands to compare in scale. The Prince of Wales – the future Edward VII – performed the opening ceremony on 9 August 1890, possibly with a sense of déjà vu, having opened Bolton's hall seventeen years earlier.

In 1895, posters appeared on hoardings in the town showing a rather alarming depiction of Portsmouth's new architectural gem being blown up. Another showed a foreign army marching down Commercial Road. These dramatic scenes were distributed to promote the newspaper serialisation of William Le Queux's new novel, *The Great War in England in 1897*. This described an invasion of England by French and Russian coalition forces, but also served to boost Alfred Harmsworth's electoral chances in Portsmouth where he was standing in the General Election as a patriot and a Conservative. Harmsworth had added the *Portsmouth Evening Mail* to his burgeoning newspaper empire that very same year and it acted as a rival to the (then) Liberal-supporting *Portsmouth Evening News*. Harmsworth was a man hungry for power and influence. The *Portsmouth Evening News* scornfully cited the Guildhall attack as an example of 'the new journalism'. In the serialisation, an enemy shell ignited gas cylinders stored in the tower of the Town Hall which blew up and crashed through the roof, crushing the town's councillors who were in a meeting (many of whom were named). The good voters of Portsmouth were not impressed with Harmsworth and he never stood for Parliament again. But, together with his brother Harold (later Lord Rothermere), he continued buying up local newspapers and, the following year, they launched the *Daily Mail*. By 1914, *The Times* and *The Mirror* had been added to the Harmsworth empire and they controlled almost half of the British press.

In 1899, there was a rainstorm during which 347 million gallons of water were reported to have fallen on the Borough of Portsmouth. The rainstorm, which lasted an hour, flooded Old Portsmouth and Southsea Common. Commercial Road was 'like a river' and boys were swimming in Stanhope Road. Water broke through the Town Hall roof and fell 'in tons' all over the building, causing great damage. No councillors are reported to have drowned.

On the night of 10–11 January 1941, the predicted shelling of the Town Hall – now the Guildhall – came to pass. Ironically but perhaps predictably, in the years before the Second World War, the *Daily Mail* and its proprietor, the surviving Harmsworth brother Harold, had been very supportive of fascism, and it was incendiary bombs dropped by the Luftwaffe that did extensive damage.

That night's fire-blitz across the city ignited by 300 raiders killed 171 and injured 430. Fortunately, the ARP wardens and firemen fighting the fires inside and on the roof of the Guildhall roof left just in time. The Lord Mayor, who had been living there, lost all his clothes apart from the suit he was wearing. The copper-covered cupola continued to blaze like a beacon the following day and it was weeks before the burned-out shell was cool enough to be accessed. A few days later the editor of the *Portsmouth Evening News* spoke for many in describing the emotional and practical loss to the city. It was 'the centre of our municipal life, the rallying point of our social activities' and 'an inspiration and an incentive'. 'The town grew up around it, and grew, too, in dignity and importance'. The Guildhall 'very really helped to make the city'.

The city council and its departments were relocated to the Royal Beach Hotel and other locations; while proposals were made to turn the shell into a memorial, others wanted it demolished in the interests of post-war planning. It was decided to reconstruct, but not as it was.

In the 1930s, architect Ernest Berry Webber, who had created Southampton Civic Centre, was commissioned to do the job. The main frontage and sides of the original were retained but the skyline was much simplified with the removal of the corner turrets. The cupola was replaced with 'an ugly short octagonal feature, nearly flat-topped'.

During the war around 40 per cent of business and shopping centre in Commercial Road was destroyed, and across the city over 13,000 properties, mostly homes, were seriously damaged or destroyed. For a population that could not go further than a street or two before encountering a bomb site, many still undeveloped fifteen years after war ended, the restoration of the heart of Portsmouth's civic life offered hope of reconstruction and renewal. Though there was criticism of its modern adaptation, the Guildhall remains an impressive

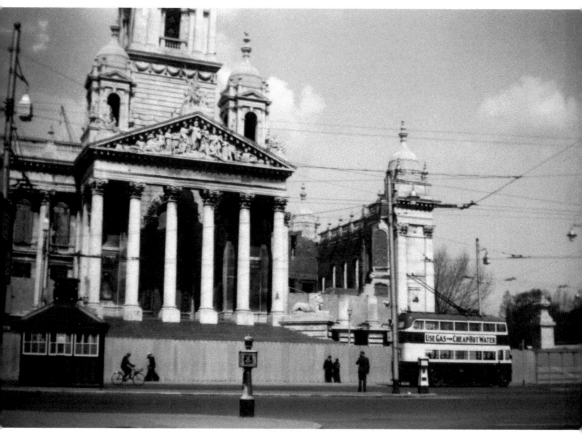

The burnt-out shell of the Guildhall following wartime bombing.

building and a source of great local pride, as well as a popular concert and entertainment venue with its capacity for an audience of 2,000.

The Queen opened the new Guildhall in 1959, and 20,000 people joined in community singing that evening. The inaugural concert by the Bournemouth Symphony Orchestra was a sell-out and the Guildhall was and remains the city's main concert venue with almost every popular post-war artist and band covering every music genre having played there including The Beatles, the Rolling Stones, Louis Armstrong, the London Symphony Orchestra, Dusty Springfield, The Who, Miles Davis, Ray Charles, Johnny Cash, Genesis, The Kinks, David Bowie, Jimi Hendrix and The Clash. In January 1972, a local audience is reported to have been the first anywhere to hear Pink Floyd play the complete *Dark Side of the Moon* album live.

Following the pedestrianisation of the Guildhall Square and its enclosure by new civic offices there was much criticism that it reduced the Guildhall's impact as a city landmark. But its five bells ringing out the famous Pompey Chimes can still be heard far and wide, and asserts its presence and our sense of belonging.

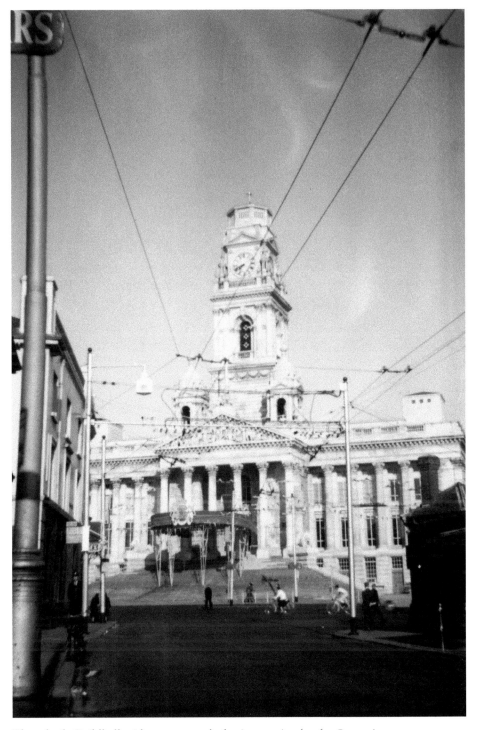

The rebuilt Guildhall with canopy ready for its opening by the Queen in 1959.

The News

When the foundation stone for the grand Guildhall was laid in 1884 sealed bottles were buried alongside, containing significant council documents and copies of every local newspaper – the *Hampshire Telegraph*, the *Evening News*, the *Portsmouth Times*, the *Hampshire Post and Chat* (described as 'a lively Portsmouth journal'). Happily, one of them survives – as *The News* – though many older residents still refer to it as *The Evening News*.

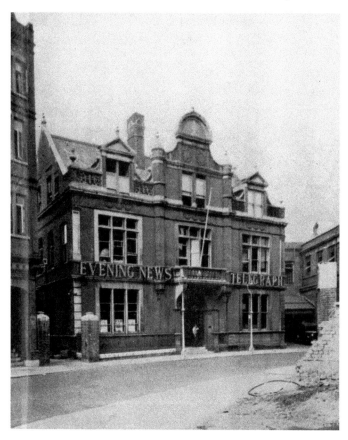

The *Evening News* offices at Stanhope Road.

The earliest known newspaper to be printed in the town was the *Portsmouth and Gosport Gazette*, which began in 1747 and folded in around 1790, and many others came and went. The *Portsmouth Telegraph*, which was later renamed the *Hampshire Telegraph*, was launched in 1799 and appeared weekly until 1976, making it the longest-lasting newspaper in Portsmouth. The remarkable longevity of the daily *News* is all the more worthy of celebration.

The *Evening News* was a bold venture. It was launched from a disused butcher's shop in Arundel Street by a Scot (who had been born in England) who could lazily but accurately be described as canny. James Graham Niven (who was an uncle of the actor David Niven) was young, entrepreneurial and hard-working.

The date was 27 April 1877, and the population of Portsmouth – those of them who had the benefit of literacy – relied on a weekly newspaper to find out what was happening in the town, by which time the reports had often become recent history. Niven saw an opportunity and launched his four-page broadsheet, acting as the editor, reporter, manager and distributor, delivering the papers personally, hot off the press, from a cart. Unmarried, Niven lived over the shop and breathed the news.

In a bedroom over what was now the commercial office, six compositors sat elbow-to-elbow hand-setting the type and, in the butcher's former slaughterhouse in the backyard, a flat-bed press awaited the plates. Sheets of paper were hand-fed into the press and 2,000 copies of the new *Evening News* could be printed in an hour. They were then folded by hand and delivered to sellers.

In early editions, national syndicated news dominated, which was not surprising considering the various roles carried out by the one content provider. Nevertheless, sales multiplied and within a few months, with a circulation of 4,000 and each paper selling for a halfpenny, Niven was in a position to employ a young man, William Gates. Gates ultimately went on to serve as the editor for over three decades and also made a major contribution in researching and chronicling Portsmouth's history, publishing several well-regarded books.

By 1883, the success of the *Evening News* was such that Niven had to warn his readers to beware of imitations. He had become aware of one that was copying his paper's style and, on one occasion, its editor had intercepted a telegram intended for Niven's office and printed it as an exclusive. Though protective of his paper and its reputation, Niven saw the writing on the wall when a triumvirate of wealthy Liberal philanthropists bought up the *Hampshire Telegraph* and launched a hostile challenge with a new evening paper, the *Southern Standard*.

Politically, Niven was in sympathy with their mission – to provide an alternative to the dominant Conservative press – and so, following negotiations, he agreed to sell out, retaining a quarter share and taking on the role of Managing Director. He later stood as the Liberal candidate for Fareham and Gosport area in the 1892 General Election, campaigning for a reduction in factory working hours, championing common land, free education, electoral reform (one man, one vote), land reform, reform or abolition of the House of

Lords, and the removal of duties on basic foods. His Conservative opponent was a hereditary baronet, Lieutenant-General Sir Frederick Wellington John Fitzwygram, 4th Baronet, an elderly Crimean veteran who lived at the Leigh Park estate. The people who were qualified to vote elected Fitzwygram, whose subsequent speeches in Parliament were almost entirely about the military and horses (he had served in the cavalry).

In 1895, the *Evening News* moved into new purpose-built premises in Stanhope Road. In 1903, the company became one of the pioneers of soccer newspapers, launching *The Football News* (later renamed the *Football Mail*, then the *Sports Mail*) which became essential reading for Pompey fans, recording, celebrating and commiserating with its readers over more than a century of dizzy peaks and desperate troughs.

By the time of the First World War, the circulation of the *Evening News* had risen to 60,000 a day and, as casualties mounted and lists were published, topped 150,000. During both world wars, not one day's publication was lost, despite paper shortages and bomb damage at Stanhope Road. The paper employed its first staff photographer in 1929. Sadly no continuous archive of original negatives or images appears to have been kept, but we are left with a rich legacy of images of Portsmouth life in the newspaper archives, their dirty graininess giving a true sense of life in the city in the twentieth century.

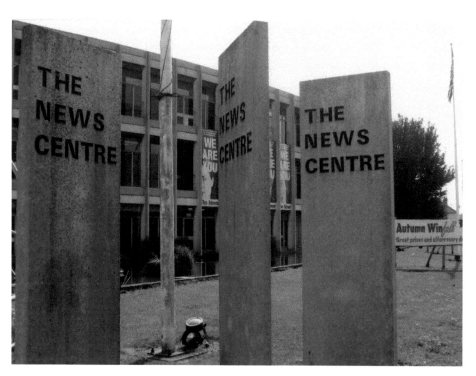

The News Centre at Hilsea, 2007.

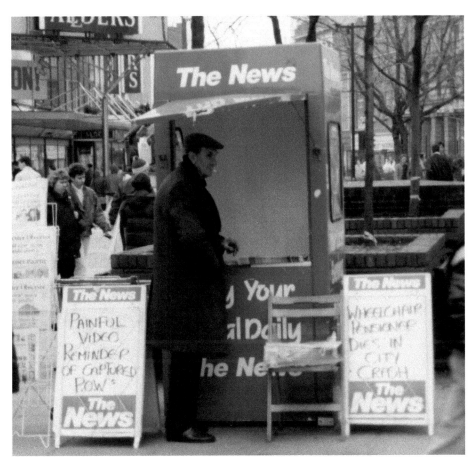

News vendor in Commercial Road, 1991.

The year 1969 brought a move from Stanhope Road to Hilsea, where the News Centre became a prominent landmark at the gateway to Portsea Island. 'Evening' was dropped from the title and a rebranded *The News* was delivered and read in over 100,000 households in the Portsmouth area. The new printing presses were capable of printing 40,000 copies an hour, a capacity that enabled the company to win contracts to print many other papers. Over the last quarter of a century, the impact of the internet on the newspaper industry has been profound; in 2013, downsizing plans at *The News* included a move to offices at Lakeside, North Harbour. It is one of a diminishing number of paid-for local daily newspapers but, happily, we can celebrate its remarkable resilience and survival at the heart of Portsmouth life, both in hard copy and online.

Celebrating Dickens

Since his unveiling in 2014, Charles Dickens has settled into the Guildhall Square, providing a lap where young children can be photographed and catching the attention of revellers emerging over-refreshed and bleary-eyed from Wetherspoons. That greatest of Victorian novelists would have been amused to be mistaken for a homeless person, but also upset that such hardship should have re-emerged and established itself 150 years after his death. He would also have recognised the immutability of human nature in the treatment of those sleeping on the street – the throwing of coins from some and of abuse from others.

The story of the statue begins in 1871, the year after Charles Dickens' death, when a committee was set up to consider how best Portsmouth should

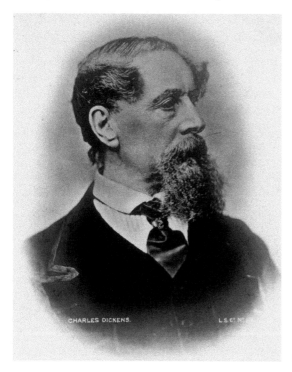

Charles Dickens.

commemorate its most famous son. Headed by the mayor, John Baker, the committee launched an appeal to raise funds and, although the type of memorial was not decided, ambitions were expressed that it should be 'national in character'; it seems clear that the committee members had hopes of something grander than a mere plaque. Advertisements were placed in national newspapers.

A few days later a *Daily Telegraph* editorial argued that great men 'need no monuments to perpetuate their fame' and that memorials are 'for the minor names in history'. Portsmouth, it was argued, 'has no call and no claim to set moving national machinery for a local monument'. The writer suggested that 'a legible and enduring slab' be affixed to his birthplace (which was then in private hands) and that, if that was not thought sufficient a tribute, the house itself be bought and preserved. Alternatively, he argued, 'let the money be devoted to some of the many purposes dear to Dickens's warm and human heart – the teaching of little ones, the help of the poor, a hospital, an asylum, or a scholarship'.

The *Hampshire Telegraph* responded immediately, dismissing the critic as 'hysterical' and 'stupid', agreeing that 'it is quite true that Dickens does not need a monument to keep his countrymen in remembrance of him', the editor continued, 'at the same time the people of Portsmouth may be pardoned for feeling proud of their townsman, and for being laudably anxious that the world should know, not that he was a great novelist, but that he first drew breath amongst them'.

The campaign, however, soon collapsed, not least because of 'the distinctly expressed wish of the deceased novelist's family that the terms of his will, deprecating in the strongest possible terms the erection of any monument to his memory, being content with any memorial which his published works might furnish, should be strictly respected'.

Twelve years later it was reported that there was 'a deal of wonder expressed' that the people of the town had not honoured Charles Dickens with a statue or bust or even, at the least, a plaque on his birthplace. A correspondent in the Portsmouth Grammar School magazine *The Portmuthian* lamented the fact that the town was populated by assorted monuments marking eminent people and historic events, but that the only Dickens memorial was 'a sculptured head and bust over the window of a private house in Campbell Road' and 'a photograph in the Public Reading Room at Landport'.

The writer urged boys at the Grammar School to subscribe to a memorial fund. At that time, the most popular author, as reflected in school library issues, was H. Rider Haggard, followed by Quiller-Couch, Jules Verne, G. A. Henty and R. M. Ballantyne. Charles Dickens was rarely borrowed. Whether this had any bearing on the amount of pocket money collected is not known, but no memorial appeared.

In 1891, Alderman Whitcombe, a Governor of Portsmouth Grammar School who was renowned for his benevolence, having paid poor boys' fees for many years, commissioned and donated an oil painting of Charles Dickens to be hung in the Town Hall. This act was described as 'the first public memorial of the great writer', but the hope was expressed at the presentation that, one day, a statue would be erected outside the Town Hall. A journalist wrote, with some prescience, 'Perhaps, in a hundred years' time'.

In 1908, another campaign to raise funds to erect a statue met with short shrift from the honorary secretary of the local Dickens Fellowship. Writing in *The Times*, Mr Louis de Wolff described how he organised a fund 'for establishing and endowing a "Tiny Tim" cot in the Royal Portsmouth Hospital' in Dickens' memory. He found 'a ready response to my appeal, just because the money was for so practical an object and not for a statue'. Many contributed, he argued, because 'they placed Dickens as an apostle of humanitarianism above even the man of letters'. The pioneering journalist and editor W. T. Stead supported this appeal for practical philanthropy. He wrote in the Review of Reviews, 'What would delight Dickens more than to see such "Tiny Tim" cots established in every hospital in the land?'

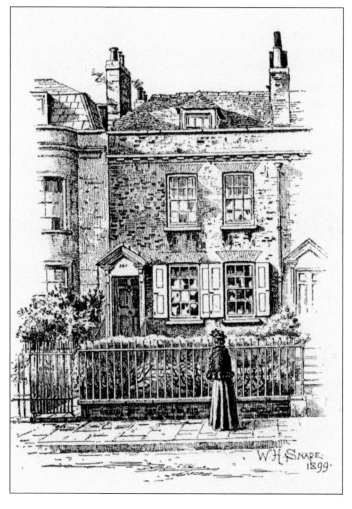

Dickens' birthplace at No. 1 Mile End Terrace.

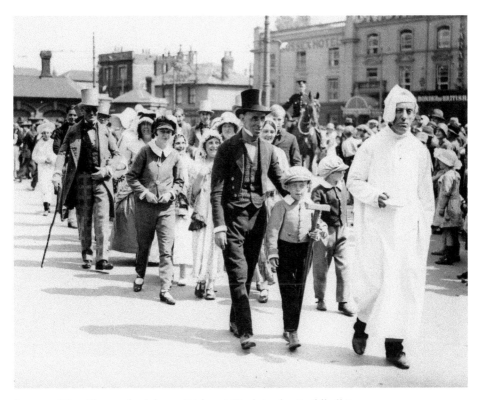

Scrooge, Tiny Tim et al celebrate Dickens' Week in the Guildhall Square, 1929.

Throughout the twentieth century Dickens was commemorated by many charitable and cultural events. In 1903, the birthplace in Commercial Road was bought and fitted out as a museum and a library for the blind. On the centenary of his birth in 1912, the local Fellowship organised entertainment for 1,000 poor local children and a tea for the blind, raising £600 to provide a nurse for those who could not afford medical treatment. In 1929, a Dickens Week was organised by local teachers which included a parade of local people dressed as his characters, pageants, concerts and a ball. Dickens fever at the time was such that, to its shame, Portsmouth City Council banned a novel based on his life – *This Side Idolatry* by C. E. B. Roberts – from public libraries because it was perceived to have questioned Dickens' morals.

On the 150th anniversary of his birth in 1962, Captain P. Dickens, a great-grandson of the author, attended a service at St Mary's Church and dedicated a plaque marking Charles Dickens' baptism in a former church on the site. In the centenary year of his death, the birthplace museum was refurbished in the style of the Regency period.

In 1976, a collection of books by and about Dickens and his works which had been built up and housed at the birthplace museum was installed in its own room at the newly opened Central Library in the Guildhall Square.

Throughout this time, the wish, as expressed in Charles Dickens' will, 'on no account make me the subject of any monument, memorial or testimonial whatever', was ignored in every respect other than the erection of a statue. In 1992, the Bank of England issued a new £10 note featuring his portrait on the reverse, and its withdrawal eleven years later was unrelated to his wishes. Then, in 1997, it was reported that the City Council, with Fellowship and Dickens family support, had approved a bronze effigy earmarked for a site outside Boots the Chemists in Commercial Road. *The Times* ran the mischievous headline 'Dickens of a dispute over statue is settled at last'.

Christopher Charles Dickens, a great-great-grandson, who could claim to be head of the Dickens family at the time, wrote to *The Times* to oppose the Portsmouth plan. Other correspondents mocked the notion that Dickens 'wanted his expressed wishes to be disregarded', and noted that he disliked humbug and hypocrisy. Reference was made to Dickens' illustrator Phiz having consistently depicted Pecksniff (an unctuous hypocrite) surrounded by busts and portraits of himself. Rather than the suggested statue, another writer observed, why not a compromise? A statue of Dickens as a toddler, as he left Portsmouth to learn to write. 'It might give Portsmouth a better perspective on its literary legacy.'

The plans announced in 2012 by the Dickens Fellowship for a statue reportedly provoked outrage, but happily brought Dickens' Portsmouth origins to the attention of the international media. The statue, by the acclaimed sculptor Martin Jennings, had the wholehearted support of Dickens' current descendants. He sits in the Guildhall Square, serene and silent, closely observing human nature and enjoying the colourful theatre of passing life and shifting times.

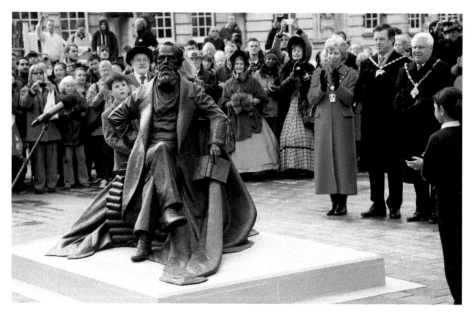

Unveiling of the Dickens statue in the Guildhall Square, 2014.

Celebrating Portsmouth's Literary Influence

If Rudyard Kipling had not spent six years of his childhood in Southsea, he might not have become one of the most popular authors of the late nineteenth and early twentieth centuries. Five-year-old 'Ruddy' – described as a 'wilful child' – and his sister were sent by their Anglo-Indian parents to board at Lorne Lodge in Campbell Road. They were in the care of a Captain Holloway and his wife, a fundamentalist Christian. As described in his autobiographical writings, Kipling was profoundly

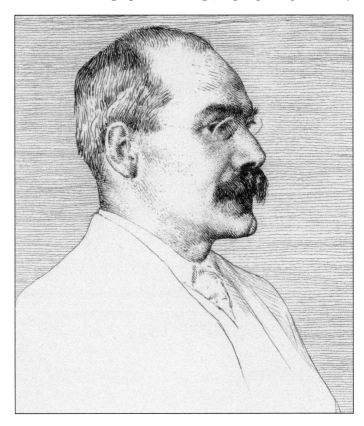

Rudyard Kipling.

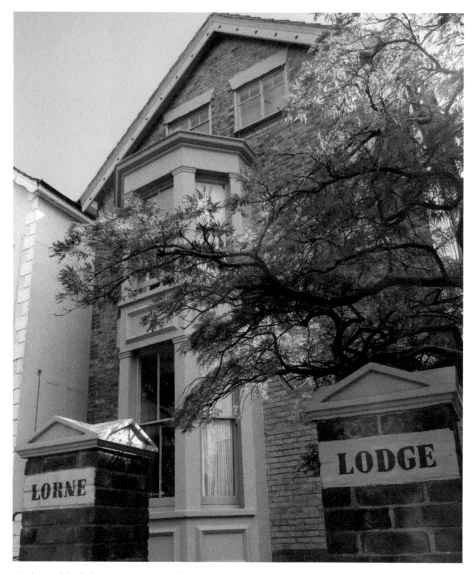

Kipling's bleak house in Campbell Road.

affected by his years there, describing cruelty, neglect and misery. He later wrote that perhaps the lying he did as a child in Southsea to avoid punishment was 'the foundation of literary effort'.

H. G. Wells' experience as a teenager in Southsea helped provide source material for two of his most famous novels as well as a grounding for his lifelong faith in socialism. Herbert was fifteen years old when he started working a thirteen-hour day as an assistant at Hide's Drapery Emporium in King's Road, an experience that found its way into his classic novels *Kipps* and *The History of Mr Polly*. Herbert slept on the premises in a bleak dormitory with fellow apprentices. The

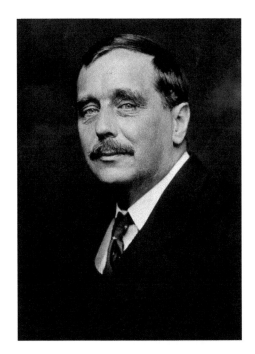

Right: H. G. Wells in 1920.

Below: Wells' workplace and home at Hide's Emporium was on the left in this view of King's Road, *c.* 1910.

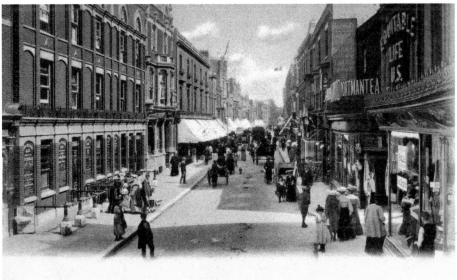

life of drudgery and fear of dismissal and poverty between 1880 and 1883 led to thoughts of drowning himself while walking along the seafront and The Hard. Fortunately, he got a grip and escaped to Kent.

As a young doctor, Arthur Conan Doyle famously set up practice in Bush Villas in Elm Grove, Southsea (1882–90) and, when business was slow as it often was, wrote stories for magazines and novels. Amongst them were the first two Sherlock Holmes stories, *A Study in Scarlet* and *The Sign of Four*. Unlike Kipling and Wells, Sir Arthur had happy memories of living in Southsea and wrote, 'With its imperial associations it is a glorious place and even now if I had to live in a town outside London it is surely to Southsea, the residential quarter of Portsmouth, that I would turn.'

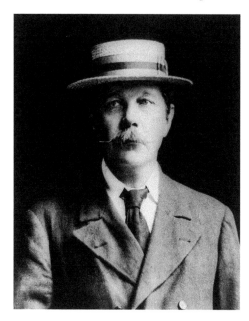

Left: Sir Arthur Conan Doyle in 1913.

Below: Bush Villas is on the left of this view of the junction of Elm Grove and Castle Road, 1900s.

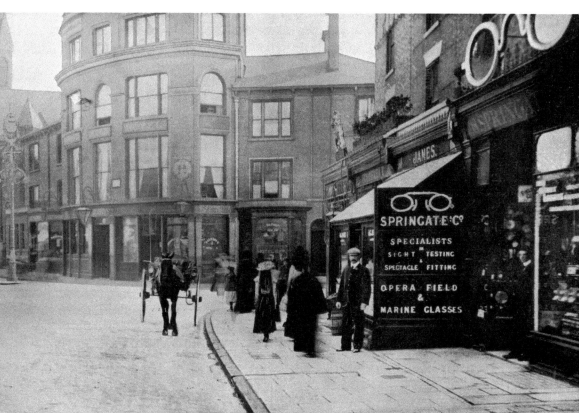

Chuck Us a Penny, Mister!

In 1954, the *Hampshire Telegraph* published a feature article on the city's visitor attractions. Alongside the well-known maritime attractions, the writer suggests that, 'if you are lucky, and the tide is out, the Hard is well worth a visit to see if the mudlarks are in residence'.

The Portsea mudlarks were not always considered an asset. Unlike the Thames mudlarks, who scavenged the river mudflats for reusable and saleable debris, the mudlarks of The Hard begged and entertained tourists by competing to retrieve coins thrown from the pier.

The foundation stone for the pier was laid in 1847. Originally built for steamships, the Royal Albert Pier was sold to railway companies when the line was extended to The Hard in 1876. The first known literary reference to the Portsea mudlarks appears in Walter Besant's *By Celia's Arbour* in 1878.

Mudlarks appeared before local magistrates with persistent regularity throughout the Victorian period, charged mainly with 'causing an obstruction', though by 1899 a by-law was in force that specifically made it an offence. Their antics were reported to have attracted crowds of up to 400 people at the height of the tourist season. The magistrates and councillors were unhappy that the initial impression given to excursionists arriving in the town by ferry or train was one of poverty and neglect. The sight of the poorest slum children begging in the mud was felt to be at odds with the civic pride that that they prided themselves on nurturing. It was the mudlarks, rather than Portsea's slum housing, that were described as 'filthy and degrading' and 'an abominable nuisance'. Their reported ages in court cases ranged from around seven to sixteen. They were fined or imprisoned if the fines could not be paid.

The editor of the *Evening News* argued that 'fines could be paid by half an hour of mudlarking' and advocated the birch and jail as a deterrent. A correspondent replied that magistrates had no power to whip children for their offences, suggesting that 'everyone wants to see the poor, uneducated children reclaimed from their semi-barbarous ways, and that is not to be done by making gaol birds of them'.

In 1890, a sixteen-year-old boy before the court explained that he 'went into the mud' to keep his mother and help 'make up the rent'. He was fined half a crown.

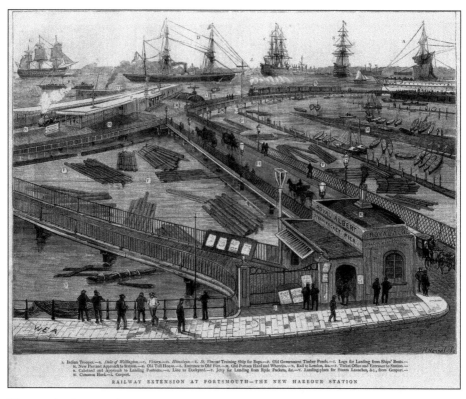

The new harbour station, 1876.

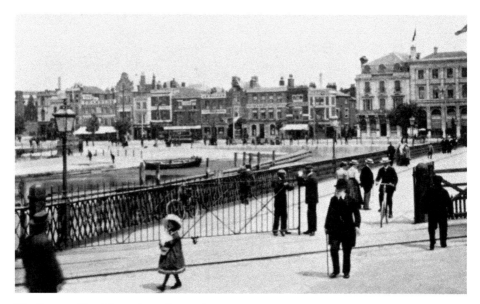

The Portsea Hard from the railway pier, *c.* 1904.

In 1900, it was reported that a policeman was to be posted on duty on the harbour approach on a permanent basis specifically to deter mudlarks, but to no avail. By the 1930s there was a cunning, or possibly a desperate, proposal to get rid of the mud, which, it was reasoned, would get rid of the mudlarks. A careful estimate was made of the cost of reclaiming 4 acres of mudflats. The project was rejected on the grounds of its 'disproportionate cost'.

It was not until the root causes of poverty were addressed that mudlarking through necessity came to an end. The post-war Labour government was the first to seriously address inequality, slum housing, health, education and abject poverty. Mudlarking continued, but for fun rather than to put a meal on the table or to pay the rent. Consciences of those in authority could go untroubled and the activity was seen as a colourful and quaint part of the city's character and traditions.

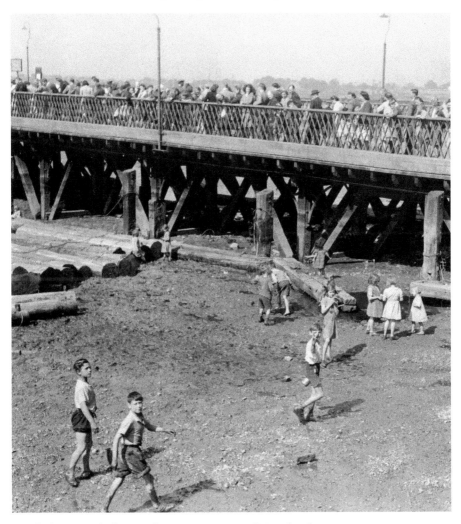

Mudlarks, one of whom is demonstrating a traditional welcome, *c.* 1945.

Down the Market

Charlotte Street was named after Queen Charlotte, wife of King George III who, on his first visit to the town to review the fleet, endeared himself to the people of Portsmouth by giving a whole week's extra pay for the dockyard men as well as generous gifts of cash to the poor and local sailors. Five years later, in 1778, he brought along Charlotte who was enjoying a brief window between giving birth to her twelfth and thirteenth children, of a total of fifteen.

Charlotte's street was developed in the centre of a large area, Pesthouse Field, which had been called Fountain Field before 1693 when a pest-house was built to isolate those afflicted by the plague. Bodies were buried in the field, or rather

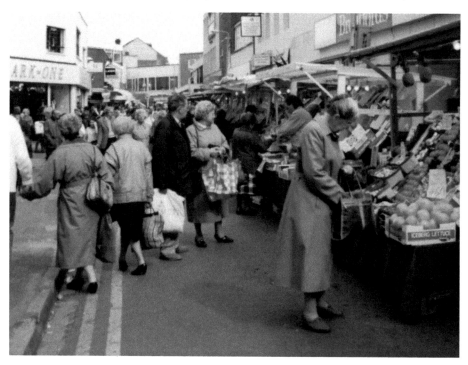

Charlotte Street market looking towards Commercial Road, 1995.

scattered according to one account. The graves were so shallow that they were 'commonly covered with crows and ravens'.

An unofficial market is believed to have been operating in Charlotte Street from at least the 1820s. Seemingly anyone could roll up with a cart, position themselves in front of a shop, and start selling from it, a situation which inevitably led to confrontation. One such incident occurred in 1868 when a costermonger was charged with obstruction and assault. He was fined a total of £3, or could serve a sentence of one month's imprisonment. Fellow costermongers assembled and demonstrated in Charlotte Street to protest at his treatment, which led to the arrest and conviction for assault of what the police described as the ringleader.

By the late 1870s, the market was under sustained attack. The Corporation Watch Committee claimed that the market was standing in the way of progress, or rather vehicular traffic. Perhaps more of a factor was the pressure being exerted by Charlotte Street shopkeepers to close it down. One market day in 1878 the costermongers were ordered, without notice, to move on by the police. They complied but organised a meeting in the Portsmouth Arms in Charlotte Street, where they complained of being prevented from earning 'an honest shilling' and made representations to the Town Hall. The costermongers, concerned for their livelihoods, compromised and agreed to limit their selling from their handcarts to one side of the narrow street, enabling access for traffic, but this was rejected, and for fifteen years there was no market, the costers presumably finding pitches elsewhere in Commercial Road or Unicorn Road.

In the summer of 1892, a petition signed by 5,000 local people urged the Corporation to reinstate the market. By this time, trade for the shops in Charlotte Street had fallen away and many had closed down, and so the matter was considered by the Watch Committee and it was agreed that a market could be held between Friday afternoon and Saturday night provided carts, barrows and stalls were kept on the south side of the street. The following month the market reopened, and there were celebrations in the Portsmouth Arms and toasts made to success and prosperity.

An account of the revived market on a Saturday night from the 1890s gives an insight into the range of produce, services and entertainments that were on show. Locals visited for the spectacle alone, for the lively and colourful theatre of the street. Stalls glowed under suspended paraffin lamps or naphtha flares and the air was thick with the smell of baking potatoes, roasting chestnuts, and whelks and cockles drowned in vinegar. Vendors' unique street cries, repeated over and again, competing against each other, were hypnotic but often unintelligible.

The fruit and vegetables at the upper end of the street sold cheaply, especially as the evening passed and perishable fruits like strawberries had to be reduced and sold quickly. The butchers did the same, off-loading big joints by Dutch auction as the small hours approached. The sale of a leg of mutton – the butcher to his assistant – 'Weigh up that lady's leg, Bill!'. The lady customer, familiar with Charlotte Street repartee – 'And you ain't seen a finer one, mister!'

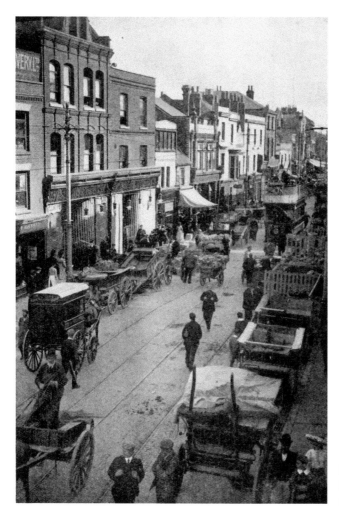

Market traders' wagons
in Commercial Road,
c. 1916.

The market was refreshingly multicultural, with 'a coloured gentleman' who would entertain the crowd from his wagon platform, pulling his patient's teeth with 'no cocaine, no gas' for free. If you were poor and had toothache there was no dignity, only pain. Having attracted and satisfied a large and sadistic crowd he would then sell them toothpaste. Another vendor, a 'loquacious chap of foreign blood', sold huge slabs of French nougat sawn from a block. In winter, 'little dark Italians' who sold hot roasted chestnuts 'never minded you having a warm in front of the cosy coke fire on wheels'.

Other stalls sold boiled sweets, books, cardigans, tortoises, chicks and chickens, tame mice, kittens and puppies. Then, at the cheap end of the street, where there were no cries or lamps, stood dark and dingy stalls with worn-out boots, heaps of used clothing and perhaps a rusty old mangle.

In 1894 the costermongers of Portsmouth got organised and formed the Costermongers' Union to help protect their interests. This was prompted by the passing of a by-law to prohibit street cries on Sundays. At the meeting it was agreed that nobody wanted to work on Sunday, but that many hawkers' livelihoods were on a knife-edge and that they needed the business to survive. It was agreed that it was reasonable, out of respect for the Sabbath, not to go within 200 yards of places of worship. One coster said that he thought the noise made by the Salvation Army 'and other objectionable people of that stamp' was much worse than the calls of hawkers trying to make a living.

The by-law appears to have been targeted at hawkers in local residential areas like newspaper sellers, knife-grinders and milk sellers, rather than market traders like those in Charlotte Street, but the costermongers of London backed them to the hilt, arguing that it was a matter of free speech. 'England,' it was argued, 'should be a land of liberty!' The police attempted to enforce prosecutions but, in the event, the local magistrates deemed the by-law invalid. By 1920 the union had gained some respectability and members renamed themselves the Portsmouth Street Traders' Protection Association.

Another description of the Saturday market on the eve of the First World War – just before noon as the dockyard men left work for their midday meal – contrasts the loud and colourful cries and jolly patter of some vendors with 'the silent old women who sit by the second-hand stalls and watch the working men picking over their stuff'. The writer is, perhaps, shocked by the poverty, but at a time when there was no welfare state, scavenging and recycling was routine and essential for survival. 'What use on earth can be found for some of the material displayed for sale is more than I can say, and yet, since these heaps of rusty old keys, and scraps of leather, and antique fragments of bicycles do find purchasers, it is to be presumed that the ravages of time have not divested them of all usefulness'.

After the First World War, it was reported that 'a different class of people' shopped in Charlotte Street, attracted because of the estimated 30 to 50 per cent saving that could be had over shop prices. A single large herring cost 3*d* in a fishmonger's, but ten could be bought for 6*d* in the market. A rabbit for the pot cost just a shilling. The range of fruit and vegetables on offer was limited by today's standards, but a report from 1925 describes business being brisk even on rainy market days, and that the produce was fresh, abundant and sold well.

Shoppers were urged to buy in the market to help the local unemployed. In 1925, a form of local protectionism was introduced with stallholders having to prove they were bona fide Portsmouth ratepayers. There were strong feelings that 'folk were coming into town and then leaving with their pockets full of Portsmouth money'.

The welfare state was some years away, and many local people suffered extreme poverty and ill-nourishment. 'Some of us are very thankful to the people who sell in Charlotte-street for keeping prices down,' wrote one older resident. 'They have saved many wives and children the pangs of hunger, and in doing so prevented much sickness amongst the people. The tradespeople of Charlotte-street are doing splendid work for the town and surrounding villages selling at reasonable prices, and I hope their fine spirit will extend to other tradespeople and reduce the worry of the housewife, who has many anxious hours thinking how she can make ends meet.'

Tensions between the costermongers, the increasing number of permanent stallholders and the shopkeepers intensified during the economic depression of the early 1930s. One resident – possibly a shopkeeper – complained in the local press that there were regular disturbances over the best pitches, audible from one in the morning through until six. This was challenged by another correspondent who was a part-time boxing promoter and fish seller in the market. He stated that there was 'a fine spirit of comradeship among hawkers', and argued that there should be more street markets (in addition to those held in Commercial Road and Unicorn Road) to provide 'cheap food for the people'. It would 'prevent big shopkeepers from holding up their prices and give the grower a chance to quickly realise on his commodity which is bound to be sold out (even if he has to cut his profit because of a glut)'. By 1935, it was reported that the number of pitches in Charlotte Street rented in one week was 1,299.

During the Second World War the area around Charlotte Street was heavily blitzed and, as early as 1941, plans began to be drawn up by the council to rebuild the city. The Chamber of Commerce – a body which appears to have been dominated by larger local businesses – made recommendations, including a proposal that Charlotte Street market and small local shops be relocated, and that flats and houses for skilled dockyard workers be built in their place. But, in the immediate post-war years, the rebuilding of stores in the bomb-ravaged Commercial Road area attracted more shoppers to the market, which thrived. By the Christmas of 1949, stallholders were collectively advertising that they represented 'the largest street market in the south of England', which could satisfy every need, 'from a pin to an elephant'. Hopes were expressed that the market should stay in the street, retaining its lively and colourful character, but others described it as 'a relic of the past' and problems with pickpockets were reported. In 1955, the City Development Officer gave an assurance that it would not be swept away in the interests of planning, that it was an important part of local tradition and that it would remain 'substantially undisturbed'.

The market survived redevelopment but on a smaller scale, operating alongside and, to some extent within, the new bold, brutalist Tricorn centre, which was reviled and revered throughout its life. For nearly forty years from its opening in 1966, the Tricorn and the market lived as improbable neighbours, but ones who rubbed along well. The cool, 1960s visionary megastructure had a confident air of permanence on the city skyline, overshadowing the transient camp of ramshackle stalls where Pompey people thronged the narrow street, treading cabbage leaves underfoot, kicking fallen apples, buying their spuds and Cox's, fresh mince and tired old ex-jukebox 45s.

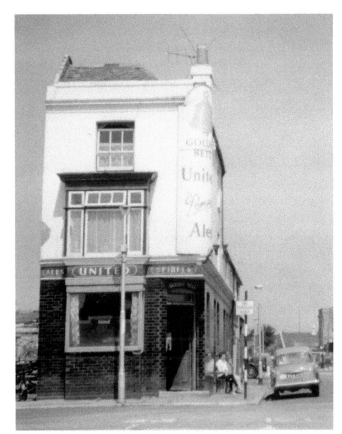

Right: The Golden Bell, a popular drinking place for market traders, 1963. It stood on the corner of Charlotte Street and Amelia Street.

Below: The market and Tricorn, 1990.

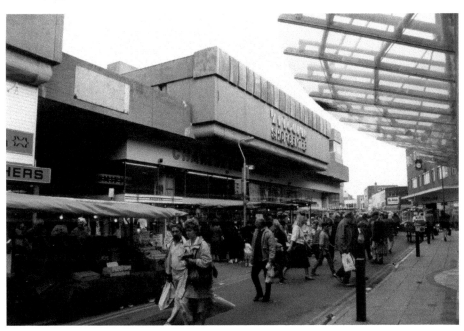

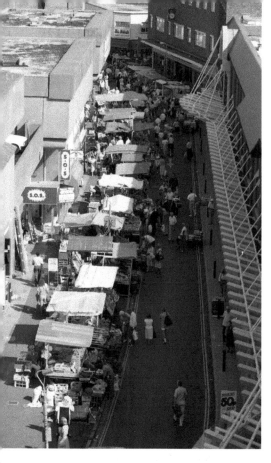

Left: Market stalls, 1991.

Below: Fruit and veg stallholder, 1995.

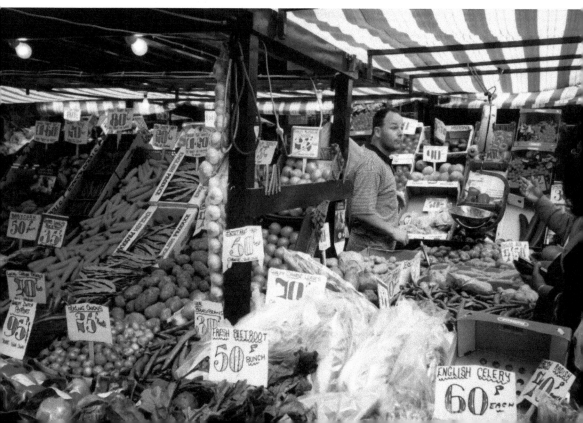

8

The Canoe Lake

In the thirteenth century, one Ralph Lumpe acquired a house with 80 acres of land which stretched along the coast from Eastney to what is now East Southsea. A fortification that was built on this land to help defend the coast against French attacks during the Hundred Years' War was named Lumps Fort; it appears in the later Cowdray engraving of 1545 depicting a dramatic battle with the French in the Solent.

A wooden watermill on Lumpe's farmland, dating at least from 1710, was later replaced by a brick-built windmill, possibly when the inlet was closed up by the action of the sea. It stood on the site of what was later called Lake View House. The area by the windmill became a small part of a large marshy area that extended along the coast close to the site of what is now Clarence Pier. This became known as the Great Morass.

At Lumpsted, or Lumps Farm, a permanent pond remained which was refreshed by the tide as seawater seeped through but did not drain back fast enough to empty. The surrounding area was not of practical use to the farm and became an area of gorse and grassland, occupied by rabbits. By 1796 this pond became known as Cranesmer or Cranes Water and later, the Minnow Pond.

In 1838 the windmill was described as having two pairs of fantails and two 4-foot French stones which had the capacity to grind eight loads of wheat per week. But later – if Walter Besant's description in *By Celia's Arbour* is accurate – the top of the mill was blown away by a south-west gale and landed in a field at the corner of what is now Festing Road. By the 1840s, the windmill, or an outhouse, was trading as a beerhouse and, despite its remote location, on several occasions the proprietor was prosecuted for serving beer on Sunday mornings – as to be open 'during hours of Divine service' was an offence. One Sunday in 1848, twelve fighting dogs and forty punters were recorded during a police raid, but while dog-fighting had recently been made illegal, the only prosecution was for serving drinks on the Sabbath. By the early 1880s, the windmill was in a very dilapidated state, occupied by an elderly woman selling sweets, and the idyllic-sounding Minnow Pond outside was 'a dismal-looking depression, strewn with rusty tins, mouldy rubbish and other abominations'.

In the late 1870s the council enquired about leasing the Minnow Pond area from the War Department, but the annual cost of £50 and the fear of the huge cost of maintenance and improvements prevented this happening. In 1883, however, a similar request for leasing the whole of Southsea Common together with the pond area prompted an affordable quote which the council accepted very willingly. Across the Solent, Ryde was building a boating lake and ornamental gardens, and it was felt that if Southsea was to be developed and advertised as an attractive watering place it had to compete and have decent attractions. To this end the council gave the go-ahead plans to create an 'ornamental lake' at East Southsea, at a cost of £1,900.

The high-class Beach Mansions Hotel (later made Royal) was built and opened in 1866, roads were laid out in Craneswater Park by 1877 and the first large detached properties were rated in 1879. A community of retired and wealthy residents was attracted to the fashionable development which stood on 'the highest land in Southsea'. When news of the boating lake plans reached them they organised a meeting in the hotel and it was agreed that the lake would be 'a reckless waste of money', would spoil their property and be 'injurious to the neighbourhood'. A retired general complained on the ground that 'the sea was quite near enough without bringing it closer to the houses'. A petition was organised objecting to the scheme and urging that it be abandoned. A Colonel MacBean said it should be asphalted over and lawn tennis plots laid out, but the meeting agreed that it should be part of an 'ornamental park and pleasure grounds' extending along the coast to Eastney. There was an inquiry and the objections were rejected, though the planned size of the lake had to be reduced. The attitude and recommendations of the residents, and in particular 'the Colonels' who led them, were roundly criticised in the local press and they were accused of lacking community spirit.

The work was carried out under the Borough Engineer, Percy Boulnois, who had been appointed in 1883 and solved many problems in the borough in his seven years in post. Unemployed men from the poorest areas of town were employed as cheap labour at two shillings a day. Grounds surrounding the lake were laid out with shrubs and flower beds and gravel paths. A human skeleton was found, put in a sack and taken to the coastguard station. Trenches were dug and two 18-inch pipes, 160 feet in length from the sea, were laid. It was estimated that the lake, covering 3 acres and 650 feet long, would hold 1.5 million gallons of seawater and that its top level would be 3 feet below the highest spring tide. On completion, there were doubts expressed that it would hold water. One Sunday in June 1886, at midnight, its capacity to hold water was tested. The sluices were opened and water was admitted on the rising tide and closed when it receded. The following morning the level was measured and there was found to be a shrinkage of 1 inch, which had been anticipated because of absorption.

The Canoe Lake and its 13-acre site was opened by Mayor A. S. Blake who bristled with civic pride at the transformation of the area, and the boost it would

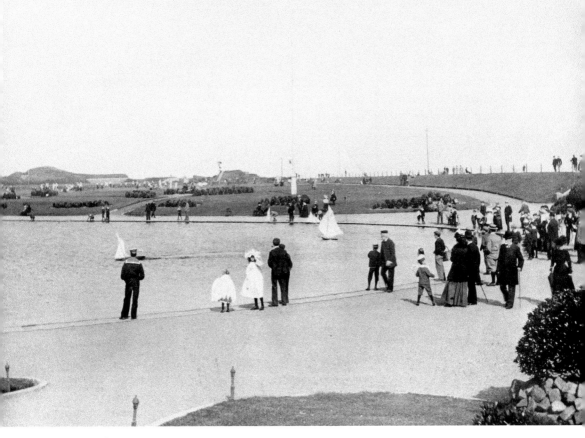

Canoe Lake, *c.* 1904.

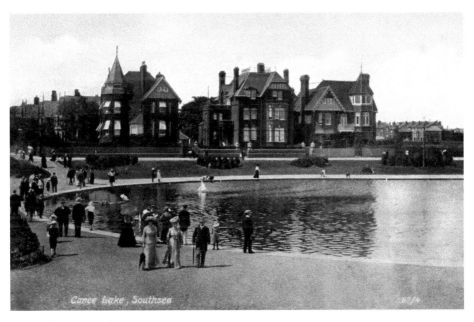

Canoe Lake, Southsea

Edwardian postcard, *c.* 1910.

have on local tourism. 'All parents who had sons anxious to have their model yachts afloat would be only too pleased to take their summer pleasure at Southsea, where they had the advantage of being able to sail on the sea, as well as enable the children to enjoy themselves on the lake. All he hoped was that young people with model yachts would not fall in (laughter).' Falling in the Canoe Lake was to become a traditional rite of passage for many generations of boys in the years to come.

Though called the 'Canoe Lake', a 1902 guide for visitors pointed out that it was 'as yet unknown to canoes', though croquet could be played nearby for a penny per person per hour. This was, perhaps, a concession to the influential residents and their concern about working-class locals and excursionists noisily having fun within sight of their villas and mansions. Less intrusive was the introduction of the most regal of birds. In the early 1900s, King Edward presented a pair of royal swans to the borough, a gift that provoked one resident to write that 'nothing living should ever be kept where the dirty, unruly children of the lower classes are admitted', describing them as having 'grimy clothes and vulgar features betraying them as the lowest of the low'.

By 1914 there were two pairs of swans living in a swan house on the lake, which was very popular with young, unruly and ruly children. Less appreciative were the 'toy admirals', complaining that the wildlife and weeds were making it impossible to sail their vessels, especially when the number of swans rose to thirty. The swannery was demolished and the swans removed but by 1958 it was reported that, again, 'the presence of swans on the Canoe Lake had reached serious proportions'. Officials accompanied by the press arrived at the lake to carry out a 'thinning out' process, but instead of the hundreds of swans that had been there, only nine birds were on the lake. After nearly two hours, three swans had been bagged and, after some discussion about what to do with them, they were released in Langstone Harbour. It was not realised that swans regularly flew between the two locations.

During the economic depression of the 1930s, a correspondent in the *Evening News* suggested that bakers should give their stale cakes and bread to the swans, a suggestion which got short shrift from another, who pointed out that 'there are thousands of poor kiddies in Portsmouth alone who would do anything to get a stale crust. We think it would be more to the credit of all bakers if they distributed their throw-outs to these starving children and their parents.'

When the lake was built there was some disappointment expressed that it was not filled with fresh water, as it would provide a regular opportunity to ice-skate in the winter, but, on occasion the temperature has dropped far enough to make this possible, including in 1895 and 1929.

Over the years, many assorted canoes, rowing boats and pedalled craft have circled the lake in exhausting circles, until their number was called when time was up. These have included pedal-boats with swan heads, introduced in the

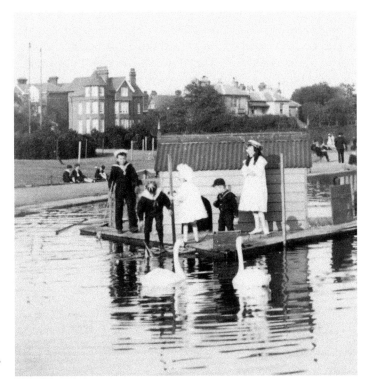

Right: The swannery in the early 1900s.

Below: The Canoe Lake tennis courts, early 1930s.

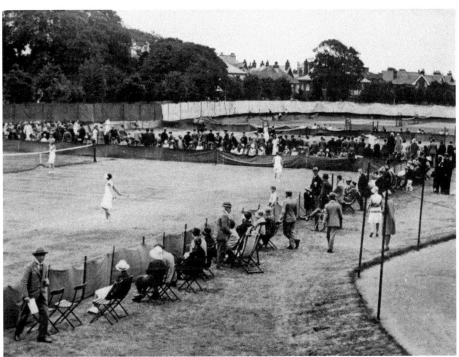

1920s, and a Donald Duck boat in the 1950s. The joy of the boats received the endorsement of French author André Maurois and his young son, often quoted in official tourist guides. 'We like England very much. It is very beautiful. We have seen Salisbury Cathedral which is very fine and the ship where Nelson died which is all gold with wooden guns, and Westminster Abbey where they crown the kings of England and the Tower, where they cut their heads off. But the best things in England are the tin canoes at Southsea.'

There was often intense rivalry, even war, between the young captains of these boats and the model boaters with their fragile model yachts. The latter complained that they had to confine their sailings to dawn or after sunset, but a resolution was reported in 1951, worthy of the newly formed United Nations, when it was agreed that they should take it in turns at certain times during daylight. By the end of the decade, radio-controlled boats and hydroplanes were competing in annual regattas. Theories were tested and experimental model boats tried out including 'a steam-driven craft powered by a blow lamp'.

During the Second World War the lake was used to carry out experiments in countermeasures against magnetic mines. Royal Marines were trained at nearby Lumps Fort for secret canoe raids which were planned to disrupt and sabotage enemy shipping in European ports. Only two of the ten famous 'Cockleshell Heroes' returned from a courageous mission to destroy ships in the occupied French port of Bordeaux in 1942.

Amenities added to the surrounding area included public conveniences and an ornate drinking fountain, with bronze angel of peace, erected in memory of Emanuel Emanuel, the town's first Jewish mayor, following his death in 1888. Nearby Cumberland House was narrowly saved from demolition and converted into an art gallery in 1931, before becoming a natural history museum while its garden became a popular and peaceful refuge. The tennis courts were a seasonal draw, attracting spectators and Wimbledon players to annual tournaments. By the mid-1950s there was a 'kiddies' corner' with pedal cars and tricycles, a 'continental café' and a police and passenger transport office at the western end. At the eastern end, Lumps Fort, following its wartime role, was considered as a site for a funfair or holiday camp. In 1949, a 'midget town and circus' offering performing seals, clowns, elephant rides and the opportunity to meet 'the world's tiniest people' possibly dissuaded the committee and it was turned into a tranquil rose garden. In 1953, the year Queen Elizabeth II was crowned, an attempt by the committee to brand the new attraction 'The Coronation Garden' was rejected by the people of Portsmouth, who were perfectly happy with the name Lumps Fort Rose Garden. A model village, built on part of the site in 1956, has proven popular ever since.

With all the attractions, amenities and improvements that have undoubtedly made the Canoe Lake area one of the most popular destinations in Southsea, it is reassuring to note that one activity freely continues as it always has – children with hand-lines and buckets enjoying the timeless challenge of crabbing.

Celebrating the Life of Spice

In its notorious heyday, the streets and bars of Portsmouth Point were thronged with Jack Tars, prostitutes, smugglers and press gangs. Fighting and cockfighting were common and every Shrove Tuesday, as a special treat, bull baiting took place. The Point was known and celebrated all over the world 'for its eccentricities', its reputation or notoriety spread by sailors and merchants.

The Point or Spice Island – an alternative name that appears to have come into usage in the nineteenth century – was an island off Portsea Island separated by a narrow tidal channel that flowed into the Camber at the Square Tower end of Broad Street near King James' Gate, or Point Gate. The gate and fortifications served the primary purpose of defending the town from the French, but was,

Spice Island and the harbour mouth, 2014.

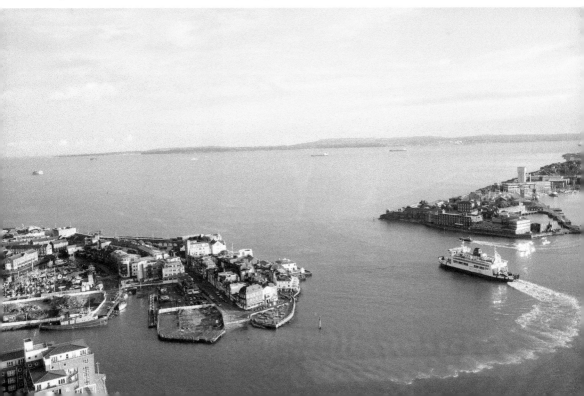

perhaps, also useful in keeping out the over-refreshed after hours. The guards locked the gates between midnight and four in the morning.

Spice Island stood outside both the town's defences and also its restrictions. In the early eighteenth century there were a reported seventy-seven unregulated drinking houses, forty-four in Broad Street alone, which included premises that were later cleared to make way for Point Battery. A history published in 1801 by Mr Mottley, editor of what became the *Hampshire Telegraph*, described 'liquor shops, contract taverns, Jew shopmen, tailors and drapers' jostling with 'Christian pawnbrokers, watch jobbers and trinket merchants; cook shops, eating houses and ordinaries' which 'vie with each other to entertain all classes, from the guests of the cabin to those of the forecastle, and whilst honest and hearty Jack is dancing with his favourite girl in the lower decks of a liquor shop, his respectable superiors are enjoying aloft, in the rooms of a tavern, the fruits of their bravery, in that style of elegance their distinguished talents and characters so eminently merit'.

It has been suggested that Spice Islanders had a language of their own, a unique way of expressing themselves, and this may also be applied to Mr Mottley and others who employed euphemisms or romanticised the area. Women who worked on Spice Island are not known to have written about it.

A guide published in 1799 suggests that travellers wishing to book a passage to the Isle of Wight and Southampton had to run the gauntlet in the taverns on Spice Island, where bookings could be made. Hundreds of watermen plied for business, charging five shillings to be rowed across the Solent, though this was doubled in bad weather. Wherries were largely superseded by steamboats in the nineteenth century and, in 1840, a floating bridge which ran along chains across the harbour to Gosport. The fare was a penny, and sixpence if you had a horse or carriage.

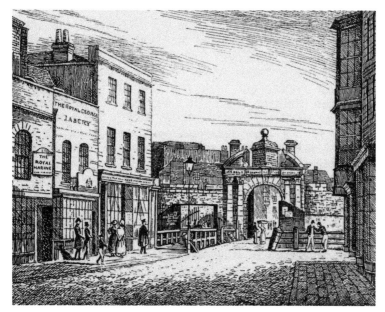

St James's Gate (Point Gate), 1800.

There are several theories on the origin of the name Spice Island. One suggestion is that spice was landed and traded there, but the most quoted alludes to the pungent smell from the Camber mud where sewage and waste from the government slaughterhouse would collect. Whatever the truth, the name has been embraced, the 'sore on the lip of the harbour's mouth' has healed and the population has cleaned up its act. Today, Spice Island attracts many visitors to its art galleries, pubs and unrivalled views of the harbour and its traffic.

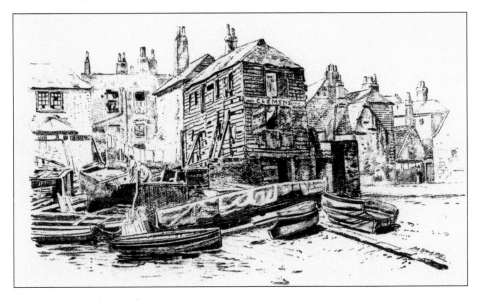

Boatbuilder on the Camber.

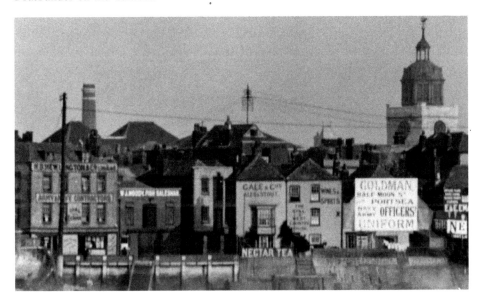

Spice Island, *c.* 1912.

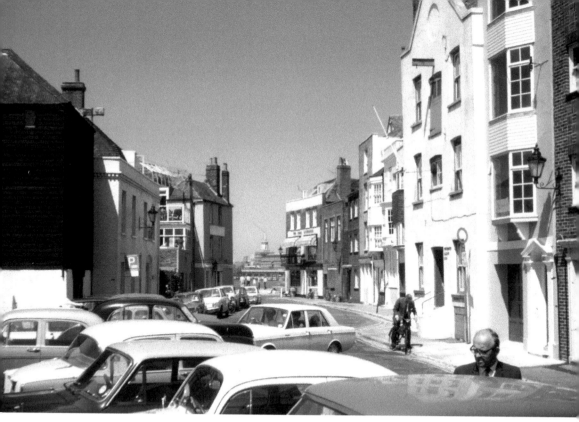

Bath Square, 1970.

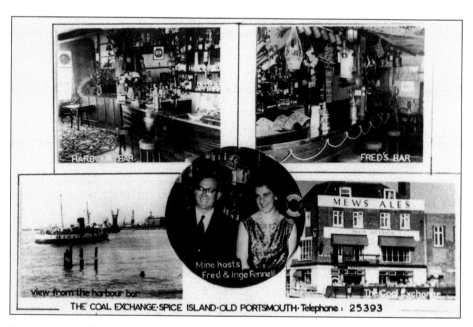

Promotion for The Coal Exchange pub, 1950s.

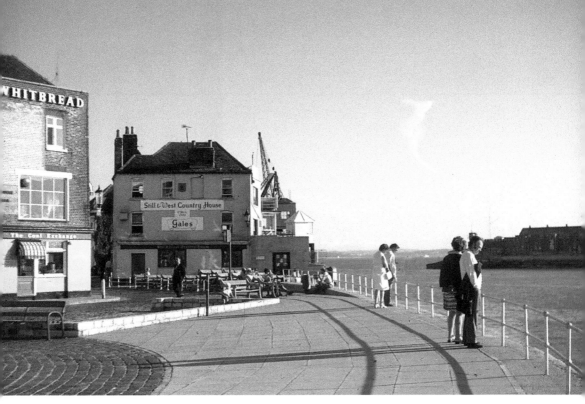

The Coal Exchange and Still and West, 1976.

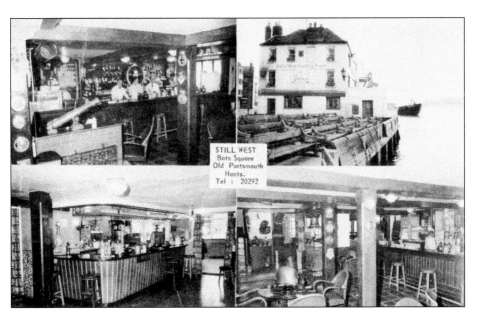

Post-war advertisement for the ever-popular Still and West pub.

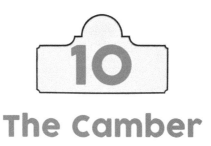

The Camber

The Camber has been known as such since the twelfth century and is the site of Portsmouth's oldest commercial docks. Portsmouth Point, the island spit, provided a sheltered quayside for merchant ships, later called Town Quay.

The Point community was famously close-knit and mothers 'as a rule bore healthy sons and daughters whose daily exercise in the refreshing sea breezes made sturdy men and women of them'. Many families were involved in fishing based at the Camber and a large fish market operated in Bath Square where the day's catch was sold by Dutch auction.

One of the Camber's other most visible activities was the unloading of coal from colliers using gantries and a concrete store that could hold up to 15,000 tons. Boatbuilding was also an important local industry, the most notable company being that started by Herbert Vosper in Broad Street in 1871. Vosper's is famous for its motor torpedo and gunboats built for the navy in the Second World War.

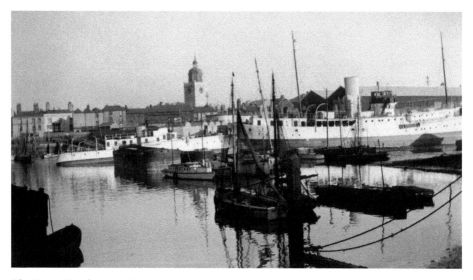

The Inner Camber, 1938.

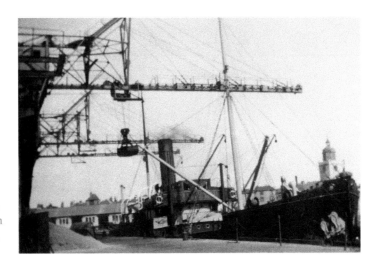

SS *Longa* of Leith discharging coal in the Inner Camber, 1937.

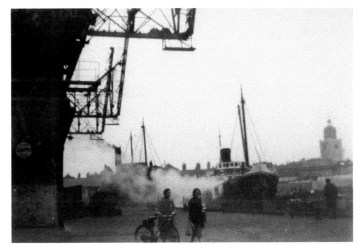

The collier *Ploglen* leaving the Camber as the steamer *Norbritt* arrives, 1937.

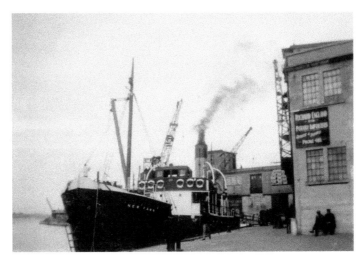

The steamer *New Fawn* discharging a cargo of Guernsey produce, 1938.

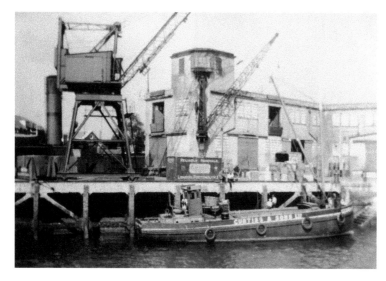

The Curtess removal company set up in Broad Street in the mid-nineteenth century.

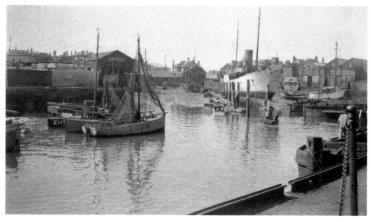

Vosper's shipyard, 1938.

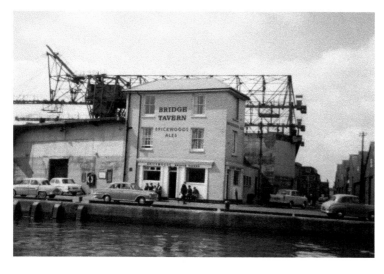

The Bridge Tavern, *c.* 1965.

11

Give 'er a Cheer, Boys!

King John ordered the building of the first docks in Portsmouth which were completed in 1212; while he has a reputation as a bad king he did get something right. Credit is more often given to Henry VII who ordered the construction of the country's first dry dock which was situated near where HMS *Victory* lies today. The first warship built was the *Sweepstake* (1497) and, later, the carracks *Mary Rose* (1509) and *Peter Pomegranate* (1509). Portsmouth dockyard remained relatively unimportant compared to Deptford, Woolwich, and Chatham, which were within easy reach of the capital. It was not until the expansion in the 1690s, when new docks were built that could cope with the largest warships of the day, that its status was raised and by the 1720s it was the largest in the country, as measured by the number of men employed there. Redevelopment and massive expansion from the 1760s onwards included the replacement of wooden buildings with substantial brick buildings, many of which are still in existence today. The ropery was the longest building in the world when it was built in 1776 to a length of 1,095 feet.

In the 1800s, a technological revolution began with the introduction of block-making machinery, heralded as the first example of machine tools designed for mass production. Further expansion took place with the reclamation of the harbour and the opening of the Great Steam Basin by Queen Victoria in 1848 as wooden ships began to be superseded by paddle steamers and then screw-driven steamships and ironclads. Revolutions in warship design and methods of construction continued into the twentieth century and, in the years before the First World War, the dockyard's workforce built nine of the navy's twenty-two dreadnoughts. By the end of the war there were 21,000 men and some women on the books.

During the Second World War the dockyard was a prime target for the Luftwaffe, and dockyard workers were amongst the casualties. By 1982, dockies were under threat of redundancy but worked around the clock to prepare ships for the Falklands War. Ships were also prepared for the Gulf War in 1991, but decline, redundancies and privatisation followed.

In recent years the aircraft carriers HMS *Prince of Wales* and HMS *Queen Elizabeth* were commissioned. The largest and, at £6 billion, the costliest warships ever built for the Royal Navy, they are based at Portsmouth, securing the city as the home of the fleet. The combined cost of the first two warships built at Portsmouth in 1497 was £230.

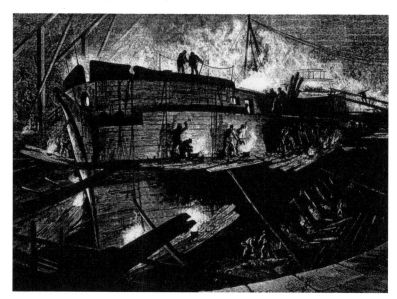

Shipbuilding in the Dockyard, 1875.

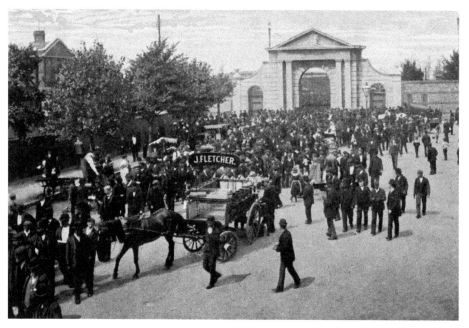

Dockies leave through the Unicorn Gate, *c.* 1897.

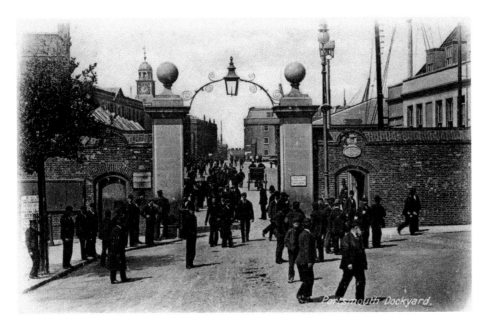

Above: The Main Gate, *c.* 1920.

Right: The old Semaphore Tower.

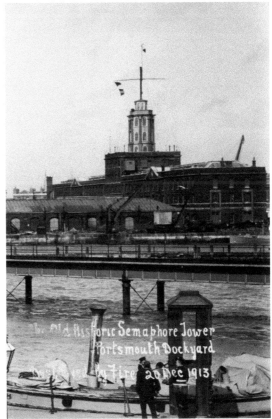

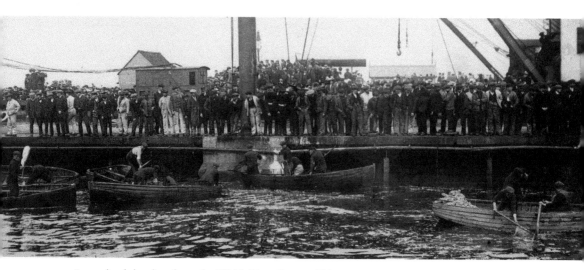

Launch of the dreadnought HMS *King George V* in 1911 – recovering grease used in the launch from the sea.

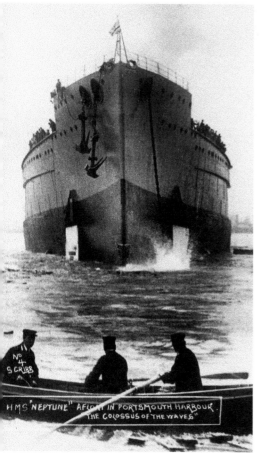

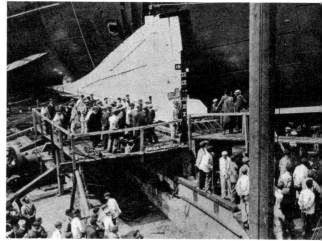

Above: View of the dogshores (used to hold the ship in place) before the launch of HMS *St Vincent* in 1906.

Left: Launch of the dreadnought HMS *Neptune* in 1909.

12

Ships Ahoy!

In 1922, HMS *Victory* was towed from its berth in the harbour for restoration and display in the dockyard and, sixty years later, the *Mary Rose* was raised and installed nearby. In 1987 they were joined by HMS *Warrior*, all three becoming major attractions in the Historic Dockyard.

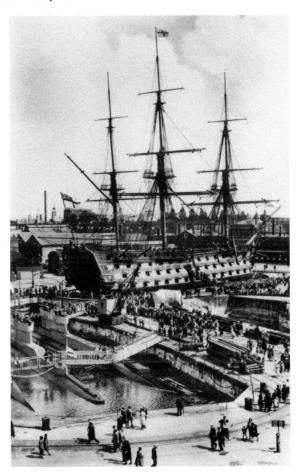

HMS *Victory*.

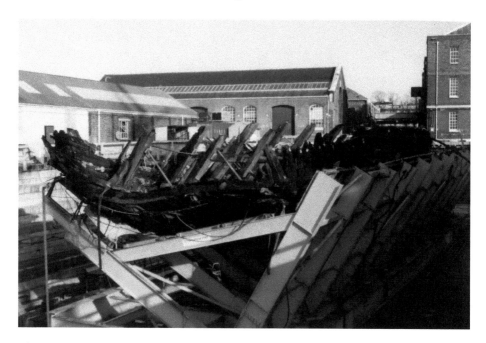

The *Mary Rose* in No. 3 Dock, 1983 – now one of the city's biggest tourist attractions.

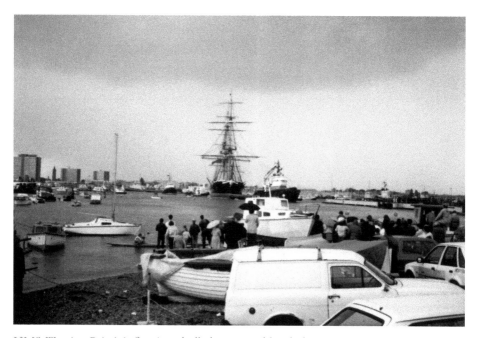

HMS *Warrior*, Britain's first iron-hulled armoured battleship, arrives in 1987.

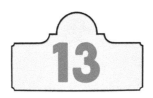

Celebrating Education
for All

What is believed to be the earliest reference to any educational activity in Portsmouth dates from 1631, when a George Welborne was licensed as curate and schoolmaster. He was possibly the first master of The Old Latin School, which was situated in the north-west corner of St Thomas's churchyard (now the cathedral). In 1652, there appears to have been a persistent problem with 'schoolers' playing in the churchyard, and the schoolmaster, named as Mr Warden, had his knuckles rapped by the Jurors of the Court Leet for not keeping them in order. In 1657, four men were fined for operating a school without a licence, and it seems likely this was Nonconformist as one of them was later charged with unlawful religious assembly. The school is believed to have closed not long before 1717 when the Grand Jury at the Quarter Sessions noted, with regret, that parents (who could afford it) had to send their children out of town for their education. They concluded, 'what a misfortune the Town is in general under for want of a Grammar Schoole'.

The seeds of what, today, is the city's oldest school, the Portsmouth Grammar School, may be said to have been sown by a teacher on the Isle of Wight in the 1670s. Richard Chamberlain was master of Newport Grammar School and it was here that a young doctor's son with an unremarkable name was admitted. William Smith would have worked hard during those long school days, receiving a traditional classical education – Latin, Greek, scripture and history, typical of a grammar school curriculum of the time. Latin was the essential language of higher education and grammar schools served as a bridge to the university.

Smith went on to study medicine at the University of Leiden in the Netherlands and obtained an honorary degree of Doctor of Medicine from Oxford University, impressive qualifications that enabled him to gain the post of Physician to the Garrison of Portsmouth. He soon earned professional respect, prospered and bought a modest farm on the Isle of Wight and land at Wymering. He took an active role in local affairs and served as mayor in 1713.

As a garrison and naval town, a large proportion of the population was transient – soldiers and sailors. The taverns and brothels were kept busy, the brewers got rich and drunkenness and lawlessness prevailed. The commercial life of the town was based largely on meeting the needs of the army and navy and the cultural life of the town was not well developed. Dr Smith would have been only too aware of the poverty of education and lack of cultural aspiration in the town.

In 1732, the doctor fell ill and knew he was dying. Possibly he reflected on his days at Newport Grammar and attributed his successful career and wealth to his schooling as, two days before his death, he ensured that others could benefit from a similar opportunity. He requested that the Deans and Canons of Christ Church, Oxford, should use his Isle of Wight estate to establish a grammar school in Portsmouth.

Income generated by Dr Smith's estate on the Isle of Wight enabled the first grammar school to be established in Penny Street in Old Portsmouth in 1753, close to the sites of the current school. The curriculum was narrowly classical, but this was soon broadened to help equip pupils in rapidly changing times. By the turn of the nineteenth century, the school was educating 'the children of almost every respectable person in Portsmouth, 70 or 80 lads, many of whom in after life became men of repute in law, physic and other liberal professions', but for the rest of the population it was a very different story.

'Education will be the curse of England' was a phrase often heard by Frederick Proctor when the Education Act of 1870 was on the way, offering free, compulsory education for all. Frederick was a former teacher and an active member of the Liberal party who went on to sit on the Portsmouth School Board. In 1930, he looked back. 'Thank God we can look around today and see the vast

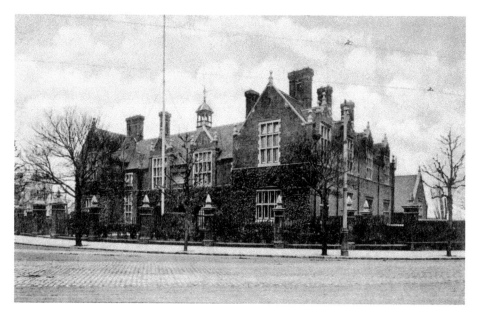

The Victorian grammar school.

improvements in the social life of our ancient city, now sailing under the banner of "Heaven's Light Our Guide".'

Before the Act, which enabled Board Schools to be set up to provide basic education for all, the great majority of the people had little or no schooling. Educating the masses was considered unnecessary and dangerous. Literacy would lead to the spread of ideas, questions, notions of fairness, discontent and insurrection.

One winter's night a merchant, a brewer, a grocer, an ironmonger, an apothecary, a butcher, a draper and a carpenter went into a Portsea pub. They came out with an idea that was to transform lives. The year was 1754, the pub was the Shakespeare's Head in Bishop Street and the eight men had agreed to form a mutual aid society or, as they described it, a beneficial society. For a small weekly subscription, members could draw on the fund in times of sickness, loss and hardship, 'supporting each other in times of affliction'. Any surplus was allocated to pay the fees for the education of poor children. Thirty years later the Beneficial Society built its own charity school in Old Rope Walk, now Kent Street. Thousands of Portsea children were taught there and, when local Board Schools were built and compulsory education introduced, it continued, receiving a payment per pupil from the government. The Beneficial Society was dissolved in 1933 and the school was taken over and run by the local authority in the Kent Street building until 1962. The building is now the Groundlings Theatre.

In the nineteenth century, elementary schooling in the town was haphazard, run by religious and charitable institutions. Like the Beneficial school, a Lancasterian

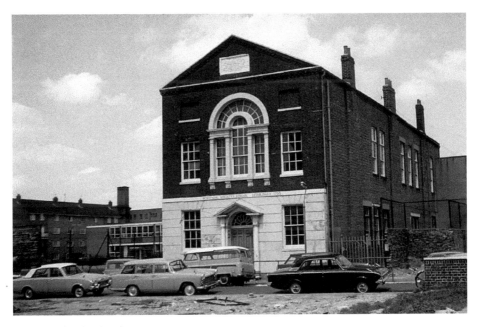

The Beneficial School, 1970.

School in White Swan Fields in 1812 and two Bell schools in Clarence Street and Nicholas Street used able pupils to pass on what they had learned to other pupils, thus limiting the numbers of teachers needed. In 1818, disabled cobbler John Pounds began teaching basic reading and writing to poor children in the neighbourhood of his workshop in Highbury Street, helping to inspire the national Ragged Schools movement, a school of which opened in Ordnance Row in 1850. Nevertheless, by 1870, there were a reported 7,000 children in the town who were not attending any school, and a large number were being sent to affordable private dame and other schools, often operated by unqualified teachers in unsuitable premises.

The vicar of Portsmouth, the Revd Edward Grant, was passionate about education and did more to further the interests of all classes, regardless of faith. By the 1860s the Grammar School was in decline and eventually closed. In 1875 Grant took the chair of a newly constituted governing body. The Penny Street building was sold and a new school built on site of the recently demolished Town Bastion. With his fundraising and motivational skills, Grant revived the fortunes of the Grammar School and is regarded as its re-founder. He is also credited as having been the driving force in establishing the School of Science and Art in Pembroke Road (precursor of the Municipal College, Portsmouth Polytechnic and now the University). His passion for education was channelled to even greater effect following his election as vice-chairman to the newly formed School Board, after the passing of the 1870 Education Act.

Compulsory school attendance, he argued, was necessary 'to bring into schools children who were growing up in a state of profound ignorance and profound vice'. The School Board accepted this by thirteen votes to one and the first

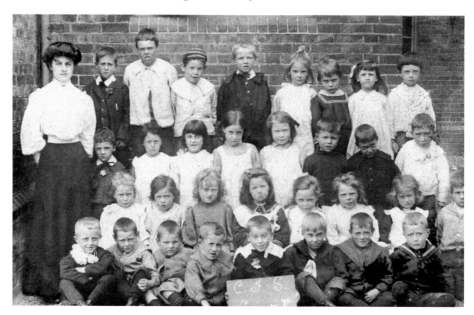

Pupils of Copnor Infant School, *c.* 1910.

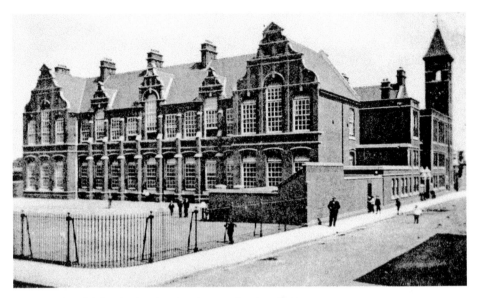

Drayton Road School, shortly after its opening in 1896.

temporary Board School opened in Chance Street, off Charlotte Street, in 1872. The first purpose-built school – Cottage Grove – was opened in 1873. Fees were one or two pence per week and a report from 1873 shows that 10 per cent of boys on the register were absent, nearly twice that of girls. Non-attendance was dealt with harshly, with truants thrashed and the parents of persistent non-attenders prosecuted. Another school serving the Charlotte Street area, Conway Street, was opened in 1875. An early log entry recorded that fifty-three boys had been admitted and that 'most were street Arabs who in many cases have never entered a school before, one-third being totally ignorant of the alphabet'.

By the end of the century, there were twenty-five elementary Board Schools in the town teaching children up to the age of twelve. Heaven's light was breaking through the dark clouds. It was not until the egalitarian era following the Second World War that fees were abolished for attendance at all state schools.

Secondary, further and higher education became accessible to all who qualified, with the availability of maintenance grants and full tuition fees paid for those attending Portsmouth College of Technology. The college was re-designated Portsmouth Polytechnic in 1969 and was under the democratic control of the local authority. By the 1970s it had become 'an institution of national repute, not only for the quality of its teaching, but also for the standard of research in some departments'.

Under the Further and Higher Education Act of 1992 all Polytechnics became universities, and the University of Portsmouth continued to offer free education for a brief period before the government introduced tuition fees and abolished maintenance grants, forcing all but the wealthy to take on huge, repayable student loans, leaving graduates in debt charged at high interest rates.

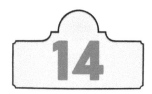

The Common for the People

In 1927, a forgettably named 'Special Co-ordinating Committee' decided that a new name was needed for Southsea Common. The problem, it seems, was not so much the negative connotations of the word 'common' – a quality that, historically, many Portsmuthians have embraced with pride – but that 'many people thought it was just a piece of common land'. The council had spent a lot of money on turning Southsea into an attractive tourist destination and this had included the recent opening of twelve hard and six grass tennis courts, two bowling greens and an 18-hole putting green. 'Southsea Common' would not do. A classier name was needed.

The council was heavily promoting Southsea as a health and pleasure resort, boasting that it had the third highest recorded hours of sun in the country. France had the South of France, England had Southsea.

From the eleventh century, Southsea Common was called Froddington Heath, a marshy and uncultivated area of Froddington Manor which later became known as the Great Morass. Dating from Saxon times, Froddington was one of three settlements on Portsea Island mentioned in the Domesday Book and, over time, became Fratton. As far as is known, 'Fratton bog' was not submitted as a proposal to the rebranding subcommittee of the Special Co-ordinating Committee.

It has been known as Southsea Common since Henry VIII had 'a ryghte goodlie and warlyk castill' built in six months in 1544, the rapid progress spurred by fears of imminent French attack. The accessible areas surrounding Southsea Castle were largely scrubland, but burgesses monetised it by charging inhabitants to take away gorse which could be used as fuel.

In 1785 the government required additional land around the castle for more fortifications and other military purposes and so purchased, divided, and enclosed the area. A shutter signalling station was erected on the common and Portsdown Hill in 1795, the first of a chain that enabled messages to be sent to and from the Admiralty in London. Messages could be sent in around seven or eight minutes but could take much longer depending on visibility. By 1817 this had been superseded by the quicker semaphore system, and a station was erected briefly on the Saluting Platform and then the Square Tower in 1821.

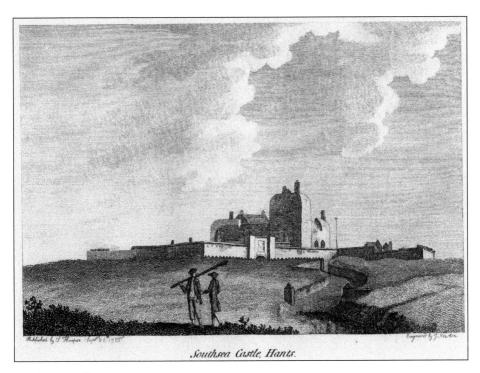

Southsea Castle, Hants.

Southsea Castle, 1783.

Over the centuries many armies encamped on the common, including Henry III's in 1230. Described as 'the finest army England ever saw', it was poised to invade France but ultimately thwarted because there were not enough ships to deliver them there. King Edward III reviewed his entire army in 1346 during the Hundred Years' War, before sailing for France and sacking Caen, with which Portsmouth is now twinned. In 1377, invading French soldiers were driven back across the common 'with great slaughter' by infuriated locals. Lastly, of course, was Henry VIII, whose 12,000-strong army gathered there to repel the French in 1545, and who became witness to the sinking of the *Mary Rose* in the Solent.

Henry VIII's army was far outnumbered by the mass of people who turned up on the common to watch a public execution in 1782. David Tyrie, a dockyard clerk, was found guilty of High Treason after corresponding with the French. He was brought to Southsea Common and hanged, drawn and quartered. Pieces of his corpse were reported to have been fought over by members of a 20,000-strong crowd, some making trophies of his fingers, toes and other body parts. Somebody from Gosport got the head.

It was a golden age for ghouls. Five years earlier, James Aitken – 'Jack the Painter' – was hanged high from the top of a detached ship's mast at the gate of the dockyard where he had committed arson. Strangely, exactly the same number of people are reported to have come to watch him die.

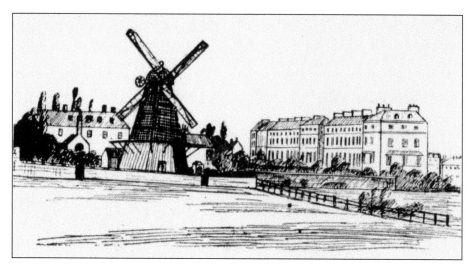

Ballard's Mill.

A windmill and its outbuildings stood on the common from at least the eighteenth century, close to the site of what is now the Queen's Hotel. Known as Ballard's Mill, in 1847 it was auctioned to speculators as being a good conversion project, with the suggestion that it would make 'a castellated abode of the finest character' or, failing that, that the land offered 'one of the finest spots for erecting a seaside residence'.

Wheelbarrow Cottage stood on the common from at least the seventeenth century and became the Wheelbarrow Castle pub (on the corner of what is now Castle Road), and the Five Cricketers pub (on a site close to the windmill) dated from at least the eighteenth century.

Southsea began to be regarded as a minor seaside resort following the granting of permission by the Board of Ordnance in 1816 for the building of a pump room, baths and reading room on the beach. Officers had returned from the Peninsular War, landing at Portsmouth exhausted, scarred and wounded, wanting sea baths to help them convalesce, and it is believed that this prompted the Board's concession. The new bathing establishment, which stood near to the site of the current Clarence Pier, became known as the King's Rooms after William IV attended a ball there in 1829, and its popularity launched Southsea as a watering place. The King's Rooms sat between the Solent, with its ever-changing panoramic vista of sails silently passing by, and alongside the wilderness that was the common.

The common was a notorious place for highwaymen who could not afford a horse (footpads) and cut-throats. Sir James Elphinstone, who served as a Portsmouth MP, said he never walked across it without his bulldog and a thick stick. But its remoteness also made it a popular venue for gentlemen to defend their honour with pistols.

There are numerous reports of duels taking place amid the gorse. In 1812 Lieutenants Bagnall and Stewart of the Marines fell out when Bagnall called Stewart a bully. Stewart defended his honour and proved he was not a bully by shooting Bagnall with his first shot. Bagnall died two days later and Stewart was tried for murder but, as was the way of the time, was acquitted. The following year two midshipmen of the Madagascar, when at sea, 'had regular disputes relative to their geographical situation'. Wollet and Kelly decided that there was only one way to find out who was right about where their ship was – after docking they would try to shoot each other on Southsea Common. The ship's surgeon acted as second to both men and was ready to mop up afterwards. Each of them shot twice and missed, but on his third attempt, Wollet put a shot right through Kelly's upper thigh. Kelly is reported to have retrieved the ball from his pantaloons and said that he would 'much rather a Frenchman had done it'.

Up until the nineteenth century, gun reports could often be heard across the common. Sometimes it was the local gentry hunting snipe, at other times proud men murdering each other. Constables made half-hearted efforts to prevent the duels in the knowledge that, if they made an arrest, any survivors would be likely to be acquitted. But duelling had become increasingly unfashionable. Famously, the last duel in which a British person died on English soil was prompted by former army captain James Seaton dancing with naval lieutenant Henry Hawkey's wife at the King's Rooms. But the duel took place on the other side of Portsmouth Harbour at Browndown, and Seaton died slowly after being shot in the abdomen.

By now very unfashionable, if not taboo, a powerful alternative to the lead ball was found. The printed word grew to be recognised as a mightier and less messy means to 'gain satisfaction'. The increasing popularity and circulation of newspapers, especially amongst gentlemen of the higher classes, meant that battles of honour could be fought and scores settled in a far more civilised way.

The furze was uprooted and the common drained and levelled between 1831 and 1847, latterly by convict labour which was also used in building the Esplanade between Clarence Pier and Southsea Castle, extended to Lumps Lane (now Eastern Parade) in 1874. Five feet of earth was needed to level parts of the Little Morass, and spoil from the making of new basins at the dockyard was used. A pond between the first houses built in Southsea in Landport and Hampshire Terraces was filled in by the Board of Ordnance in 1836 and a large brick building called the Firebarn, used for storing munitions to support Southsea Castle, was demolished in 1859.

An avenue of trees stretching on the common from Castle Road to Osborne Road was planted in 1866, paid for by Alderman Emanuel who had been elected the first Jewish mayor. Known as 'Emanuel's Grove', it provided shade and shelter to promenaders and was a popular 'lovers' walk', so much so that complaints of indecent behaviour and fear for the moral welfare of young people led to the council ordering the trees to be cut down, much to the disappointment of romantics.

Southsea Common as a place for risqué encounters was the starting point for a musical play, *The Queen's Shilling*, premiered in 1879. The high-society heroine, Kate, the daughter of a general with a reputation for 'fun and frolic', is promenading on the common 'masquerading as a singing girl' with her maid. Soldiers, the reviewer notes, 'are not refined in their method of love-making' and when some 5th Lancers pay attention to Kate's maid it all becomes 'highly embarrassing'. But a young private called Dick comes to the rescue, and things carry on from there. It was well reviewed and the Kate character 'scored in her duet with Dick'.

While the well-to-do were enjoying light operatic entertainments, pampering themselves in the King's Room, or killing each other in waistcoats, the grim reality for the majority of the population was that life was a hard and relentless struggle to survive, and this was reflected in life on the common. The gorse may have been cleared and a level playing field created but it was still a jungle out there. The welfare state was a whole century away.

The common was, according to a local newspaper editorial, 'a practical no-man's land where all may do as they please'. It certainly became a popular location for importuning by 'common prostitutes', affording a good panoramic view that meant that any advancing constables could be spotted in good time. The police countered by dressing in plain clothes and, it appears, entrapping women. 'The Southsea Common Nuisance', as the press described the problem,

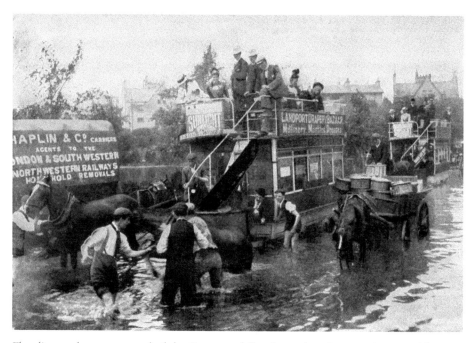

Flooding at the western end of the Common following a thunderstorm in 1899. The water was reported to be up to 5 feet deep in places.

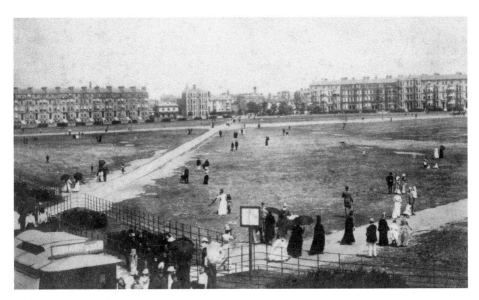

The Common in the 1890s.

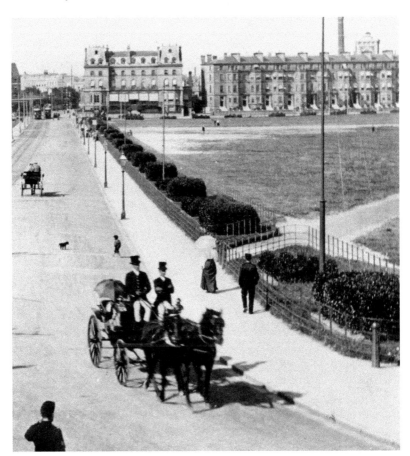

Pier Road
and the
Common,
1904.

was especially shocking because it took place in aspiring, respectable upmarket Southsea, a place that was trying to attract developers, investment and wealth, as well as visitors with money to boost the local economy and enjoy the new municipal attractions. The Ladies' Mile had become a popular place to promenade in gowns with gay parasols in the summer. If women did their business in their own rented Voller Street slum, in a Queen Street back alley or at the Devil's Acre, then it seemed less of an issue, or at least less visible to those good, respectable people who lived in safety and comfort and did not want to be reminded of the dark side.

Convicted women were sometimes invited by the magistrate to leave the town, but almost invariably they were imprisoned for a week or a fortnight, sometimes with hard labour, depending on whether they were regular offenders. One such, Theresa King, at the age of thirty-five, was caught on the common and sentenced to seven days in 1892. Over two years later, and still at the age of thirty-five, she appeared again and received fourteen days with hard labour.

Pimps were reported to congregate on the corner of Kent Road every evening, 'waiting to share the proceeds of the immorality of women who prowled about the common and accosted passers-by'. It is worth noting that, while the pimps are described as 'loafers', it is the women who are 'immoral' and 'prowl' and 'accost'. There is little sense, over the years, of those men looking to pay for sex with a prostitute having any agency. This was not the case in the post-war years when gay men from all walks of life and all uniformed services, including a war veteran and a Salvation Army officer, were enthusiastically trapped by undercover policemen and prosecuted for 'importuning for immoral purposes'.

By the late nineteenth century, in the heyday of the British Empire, the sights and sounds of military displays, training, drills and inspections became a part of the spectacle and character of the rapidly growing Southsea. In 1884, the local authority leased the common, but the military retained its control and access over its use which prevented rapacious Victorian speculators developing along the line of the shore. Consequently, the seafront houses and hotels were built overlooking the common with a Solent view beyond.

A guidebook from 1896 describes 'a wide common' where 'frequent reviews and marches past' take place. 'It is very seldom that it is entirely free from soldiers, some drilling, some signalling, others surveying, others looking on at those working'. Recruits to the Portsmouth battalions drilled on the common before being sent to fight in the First World War, and anti-aircraft batteries sited there defended the city against the Luftwaffe in the Second.

Money paid for investment in war loans helped enable the council to purchase the common from the War Department in 1923 for £45,000 and a clause was inserted to prevent the Corporation from building on the western part. Improvements could now begin in earnest, with flower beds along the roadsides, tennis courts, bowling greens, a children's boating lake and paddling pool. In the late 1920s, a triangular piece of the land east of Southsea Castle was turned into a

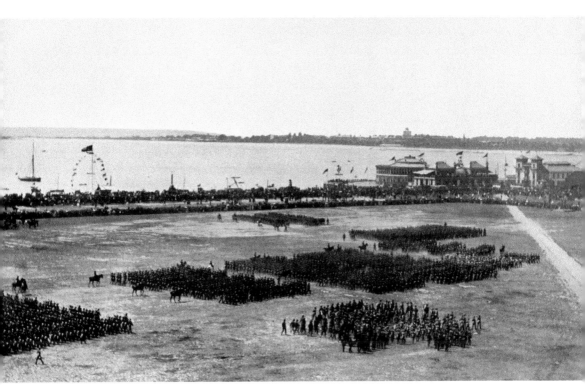

Military drilling, *c.* 1904.

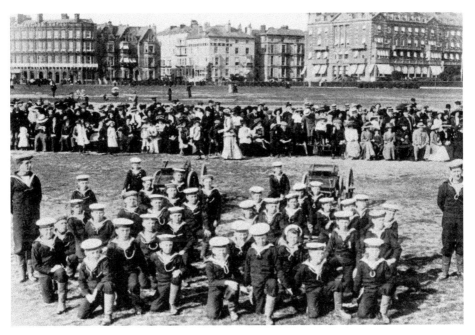

Naval display, *c.* 1904.

sunken, sheltered area where exotic birds and shrubs were nurtured in aviaries and around the rocks. Later additions were an illuminated fountain and, in 1948, the Rock Garden Pavilion which served for many years as a popular café and dance venue. It was closed in 1986 and was replaced by the indoor leisure complex, the Pyramids, which opened in 1988, though the rock garden remains.

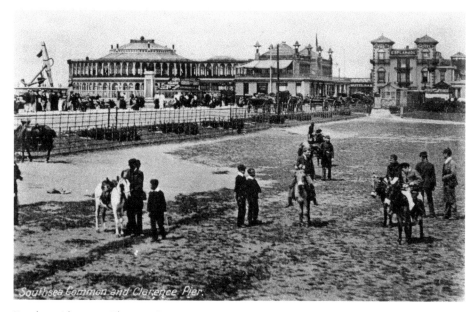

Donkey rides near Clarence Pier, *c.* 1914.

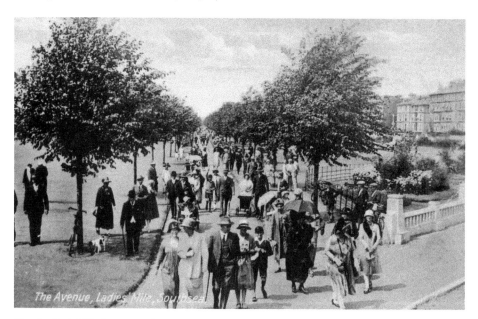

The Ladies' Mile between the wars.

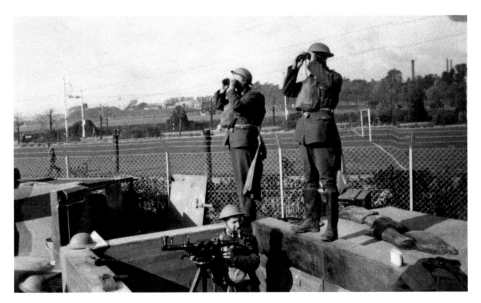

Ever-vigilant men of the 57th Heavy Anti-Aircraft Battery on Southsea Common, autumn 1939.

In the summer of 1939, a floral clock was added as another attraction, inspired by one in Edinburgh which had gained national attention. Located in front of the Southsea Castle café, it measured 18 feet in diameter, had bevel gears and a special motor. Flowers bloomed on the hands which were set in a circular flower bed with the message 'Southsea for the Best Time' spelled out in bright colours. Unfortunately the Second World War, declared a few weeks later, prevented good times in the blitzed city for several years, but the clock became a popular tourist attraction after the war, featuring in many holiday snaps. The flowers were always well maintained, though the time shown became increasingly inaccurate.

Long hopes for a bandstand were satisfied by the end of the 1920s, when the sound of military bands could be heard on the breeze across the common asserting a fondness for being beside the seaside. It was put to novel use in 1929 when, at a time when few households had wirelesses (radios), a running commentary on the FA Cup final was broadcast from there. By the 1950s the bandstand had been absorbed into a roller-skating rink and it is now Southsea Skatepark.

The Southsea Miniature Railway by Southsea Castle opened in 1931 with three-quarters of a mile of track, and the sight and sound of steam and whistle was an immediate hit, attracting over 50,000 young passengers during the 1932 season. But after many changes in gauge and locomotives, it was closed in 1989.

The D-Day Museum was opened in 1984 by the Queen Mother and tells the story of Operation Overlord during the D-Day landings at Normandy in 1944. A landing craft that landed at Gold Beach in the D-Day assault was restored and put on permanent display under a canopy beside the museum in 2020.

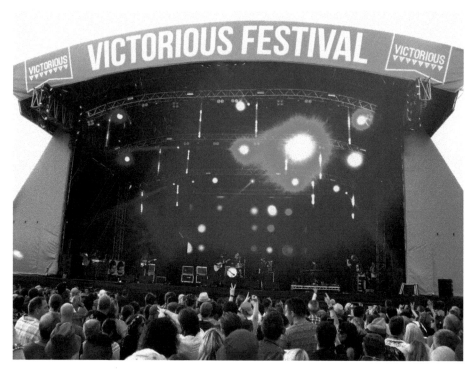

Victorious music festival, 2016.

Post-war, the common has continued to be used for the benefit of the city in many diverse and imaginative ways: athletic displays; royal agricultural shows; county lacrosse; cricket; circuses; kite festivals; music festivals; the Radio 1 roadshow; vintage car, bus and military vehicle rallies; religious rallies; fairs; heavy horse rallies; VE and D-Day anniversary events; and as a destination of demonstrators marching from the Guildhall.

The survival of the largest part of the common is due to the historic demands of the military to maintain a clear range of fire from the harbour defences at attacking ships along the coastline. Despite the council's ambitious tourist attraction plans between the wars, Dutch elm disease in the 1970s, the Great Storm of 1987 and mass barbecuing, the common remains a constant. The area is fenced-off and monetised regularly on a larger scale than ever, but the ticketed events that have been organised have proven immensely popular, such as the joyous Victorious music festival, held on the common since 2014. All these things have taken their toll on, or chipped away at, the beauty and free accessibility of this special place, but the common remains a much-loved and vital green breathing space in our densely populated island city.

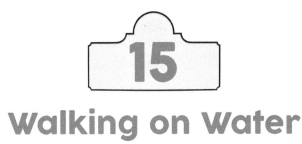

Walking on Water

The *Portsmouth Times* reported in 1865 that 'the celebrity which Southsea has obtained as an attractive watering place has directed the attention of a number of enterprising gentlemen, among whom are many of our townsmen, who are deeply interested in the prosperity of the borough, to the necessity of providing adequate accommodation for visitors ...'

The 'prosperity of the borough' also benefited many councillors and aldermen who sat on the boards of local companies set up to build and service the new attractions. In this case, the luxurious Beach Mansions hotel was being opened for wealthy visitors to enjoy the sea views, breathe in the ozone, and be even more pampered than usual.

The panoramic view of the Solent was missing something and so, in 1877, it was announced that a new 'elegant but substantial structure' would be built which would enable visitors to walk on water. Following consent granted by the Admiralty – which had recently asserted its rights to the land between high and low water marks – tenders were invited, the contract was awarded and the first pile driven (actually screwed) in June 1878. It was built privately by the South Parade Pier Company, whose board, again, was made up of local businessmen and 'our townsmen'.

On a wet July day in 1879, the wife of the then Lt Governor of the garrison, Princess Edward of Saxe-Weimar, cut a blue ribbon and broke a bottle on a girder. The pier was unfinished, but everyone agreed that, when it was, it would be a boon to Southsea. The length of the pier was reported to be around 600 feet and the breadth at the pier head around 150 feet. The editor of the *Evening News* congratulated the company on what was bound to be a major attraction, especially when the planned tramway connection was made. Initially functioning as a disembarkation point for Isle of Wight steamers, within a few years a pavilion and concert hall had been added, the trams were running, and visitors queued along the pier for regular pleasure trips by steamer from the pier head.

The 'Merry Makers' were performing on the stage on the afternoon of 19 July 1904 when their audience suddenly left, prompted by a shout of 'Fire!'. The performers attempted to retrieve their own belongings from the dressing room

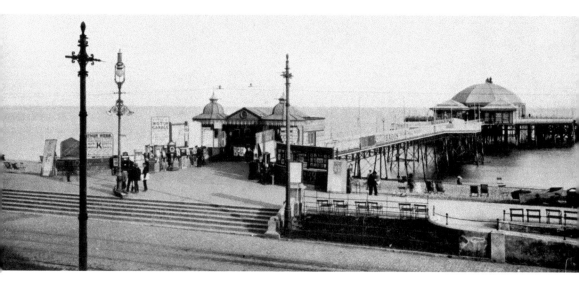

The original South Parade Pier with pavilion and concert hall, *c.* 1900.

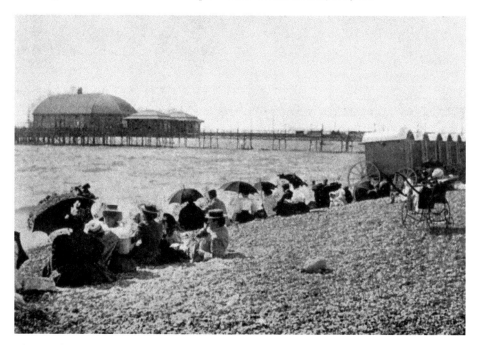

The pier from Southsea beach, *c.* 1900.

but were bundled out just in time. Within thirty minutes the roof of the pavilion had been engulfed by flames and crashed in. The pier head was destroyed, leaving blackened, twisted girders and pillars. Portsmouth's three fire engines were on the scene quickly but the fire was so rapid and intense there was little they could do. Miraculously, there were no casualties.

Unlike the 'Merry Makers' and other artists, the pier was fully insured. A charity relief fund was launched for the performers who lost costumes and instruments, and for pier staff who were now unemployed. The wrecked pier was neglected for several years before being bought by the Corporation. Other local authorities successfully ran their own municipal piers, like Bournemouth and Brighton, and £70,000 was spent on the purchasing and construction of a grand new pier, which opened in 1908.

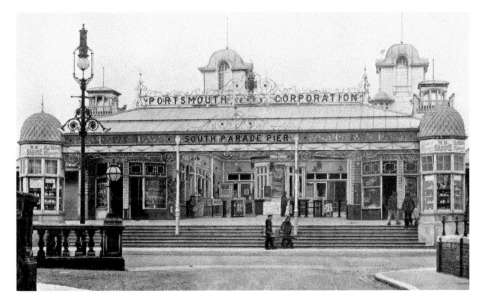

Above: The new pier, *c.* 1908.

Right: Promenaders, the pier's bandstand and a departing steamer, *c.* 1908.

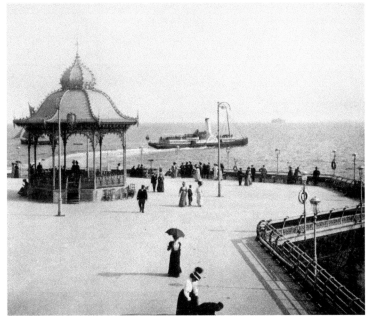

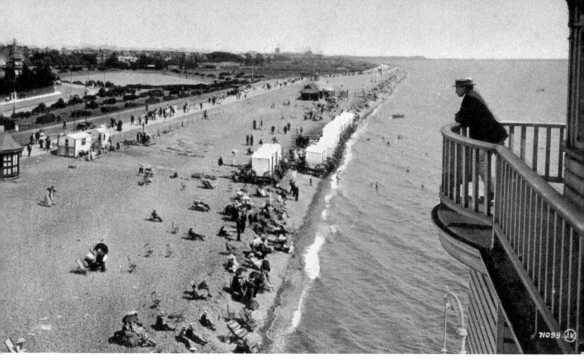

A postcard view from the pier in Edwardian days.

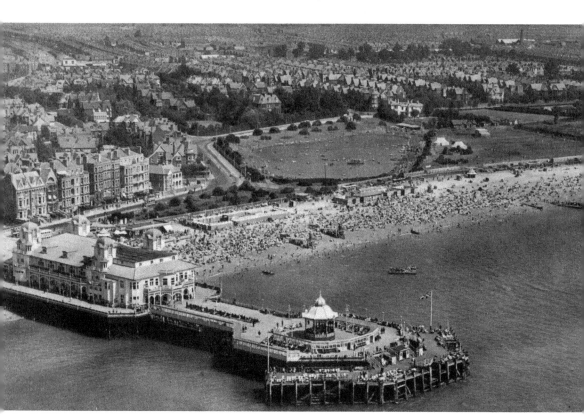

The pier and Canoe Lake, *c.* 1932.

The White Palace, as it was named in the press, was designed by the lively and talented local architect G. E. Smith, and imparted a feeling of 'comfortable festivity'. A spacious pavilion housed a hall which served as a café during the day and a dance hall in the evening. A theatre, which could seat 1,100 on the ground floor and 600 in the balcony, was later described as 'an Edwardian gem, gilt and plush'. The promenade deck was made of fireproof material, and an octagonal landing stage for pleasure steamers was overlooked by an illuminated bandstand at which a resident orchestra played, around which was a dance or roller-skating area.

Ferry services to Cherbourg were being offered in 1937, though this service was not to last. In 1939, a record number of visitors – 130,000 – passed through the pier turnstiles during the August bank holiday on the eve of war.

The pier closed down after the outbreak of war and was requisitioned for the preparation and embarkation of troops to France. It was adapted to cope with the large numbers by the addition of scaffolding and temporary piers enabling quick access to landing craft. For many men who were soon to fight on the D-Day beaches, stepping off the pier was the last piece of England they would know.

The post-war period was a boom time for the pier, with top acts like Joe Loss and his orchestra, Nat Gonella, Harry Secombe, Petula Clark, Shirley Bassey, Flanagan and Allen, Frankie Howerd, Tommy Steele and Portsmouth-born Peter Sellers. In the 1953 season, visitors exceeded one million.

Fires broke out in the pavilion in 1954 during an organ recital and again in 1966 during rehearsals for a variety show. The theatre was removed the following year and the entire enterprise leased to Trust House Forte. This had the advantage of attracting bands like Free, T-Rex, the Velvet Underground, Pink Floyd, Genesis and David Bowie. But in 1974, another fire, ignited during the filming of Ken Russell's rock opera *Tommy* in the ballroom, destroyed a large part of the pavilion. Oliver Reed and 200 extras who were in the ballroom made it to safety, though some were reported to have jumped into the sea to escape the flames. Again, there were no casualties.

The pavilion was rebuilt on a smaller scale and has continued to host bands, folk festivals, discos, comedy acts and club nights. Ownership of the pier changed hands several times and, in recent years, it has been restored. For nearly 150 years, South Parade Pier has entertained audiences, attracted anglers and exercised promenaders. But another uncelebrated constant throughout that time is the popularity of the dark area of beach beneath for amorous liaisons.

No such opportunities are available at Clarence Pier, the first pier to be built at Southsea. Opened as Clarence Esplanade Pier in 1861, in its original form it was little more than a landing stage for steamboats to Ryde, though on its first day of opening 800 people paid a toll simply for the novelty of walking on it. It was extended in 1874 and a grand domed pavilion and ornate entrance opened in 1882 offering entertainments that were a far cry from those offered on the site today. It was destroyed in the blitz of 10 January 1941, which also claimed the Guildhall.

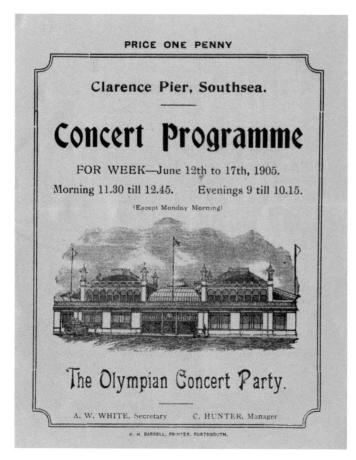

Left: Clarence
Pier entertainment
programme, 1905.

Below: Clarence
Esplanade and Pier,
c. 1904.

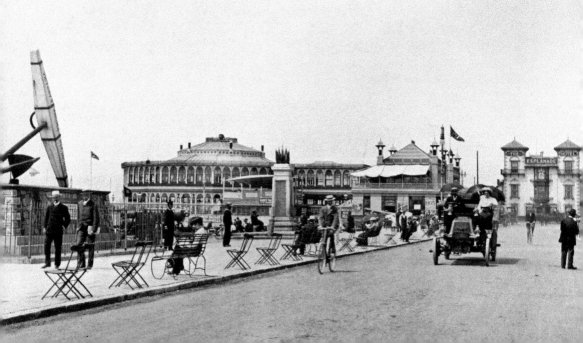

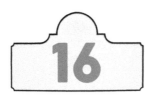

16

Play up Pompey!

At the heart of Portsmouth is its football club, established in 1898 by five businessmen. They shrewdly bought 5 acres of vacant land within walking distance of Fratton railway station for £4,950. The pitch was laid out, stands erected, a manager and players recruited and then it all kicked off. Over a century later, a journalist wrote that 'watching Portsmouth is a bit like living with the possibility of overwhelming moments of pleasure and the absolute guarantee of pain'.

Surrounded by tight, terraced houses, Fratton Park is a friend, a noisy neighbour, a place of worship. For one match in 1939, its turnstiles clocked up a then-record crowd of 47,614. Pompey went on to win the FA Cup that year before fixtures were suspended at the outbreak of war. They were League Champions of England in 1948–49 and 1949–50, and the attendance record was broken again on 26 February 1949 when an improbable and possibly hazardous crowd of 51,385 fans was crammed in. The turnstiles had to be closed eighty minutes before kick-off and a disappointed crowd gathered outside where a sympathetic police sergeant gave them a running commentary.

Nearly half a century later an estimated 150,000 people lined the streets of Portsmouth and gathered on Southsea Common to welcome the Blue Army, following their FA Cup win of 2008. The Pompey Chimes filled the city.

Pompey captain Jimmy Guthrie receives the FA Cup from the King at Wembley, 1939.

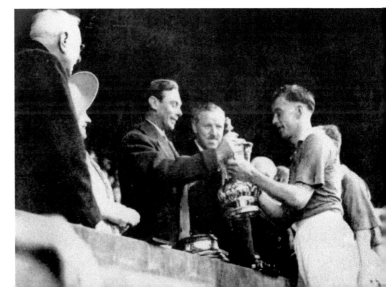

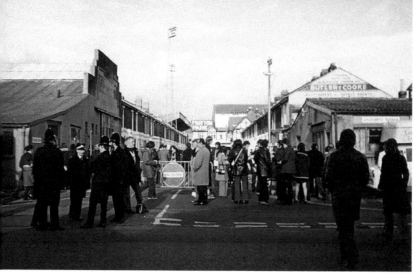

Frogmore Road on match day, 1974.

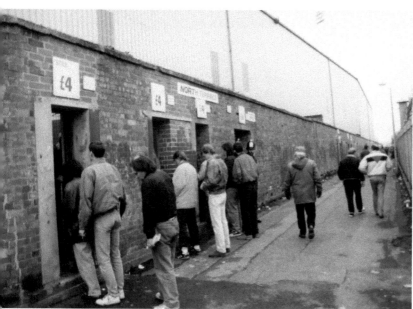

The turnstiles in 1991.

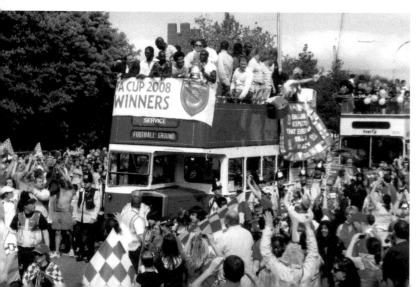

The victorious Pompey team en route to a mass reception on Southsea Common in 2008.

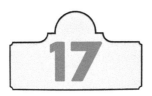

17

Spinnaker Tower

The Spinnaker Tower represents a remarkable feat of engineering and has established itself as a symbol of Portsmouth, supplanting, for some, HMS *Victory* or the Guildhall. The great Victorian engineer Isambard Kingdom Brunel was born a few hundred metres away from where the iconic landmark stands, soaring 557 feet (170 metres) above the harbour, dominating the Solent and the city; he would have been impressed. The total length of piling used was over 2 miles, one of them the height of Nelson's column. The total amount of concrete used would fill five and a half Olympic-sized swimming pools, the bows are formed from 1,200 tonnes of structural steel and the 27-metre spire weighs 14 tonnes. It was to be called the Millennium Tower but it opened five years late, on 18 October 2005. In the years since there have been technical problems, but it remains a popular iconic structure, impressive both to look at, and to look from – the harbour, the city and beyond. The official name of the tower has varied according to ill-advised sponsorship deals, but to locals it will always remain simply 'the Spinnaker'. Expert engineering has ensured that, despite the sail that gives it its name, the tower remains largely where it was built in high winds, with the tower flexing up to 6 inches (150 mm).

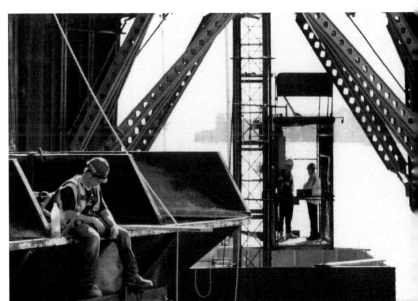

Building the
Spinnaker, 2003.

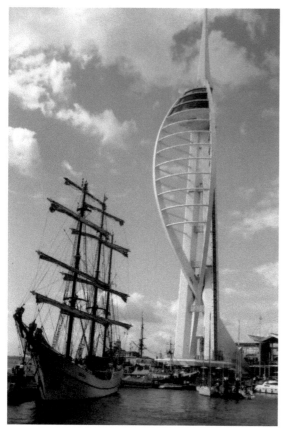

Left: The Spinnaker, 2010.

Below: The Spinnaker, Gunwharf and Camber at sunset, by Tony Hicks, 2020.

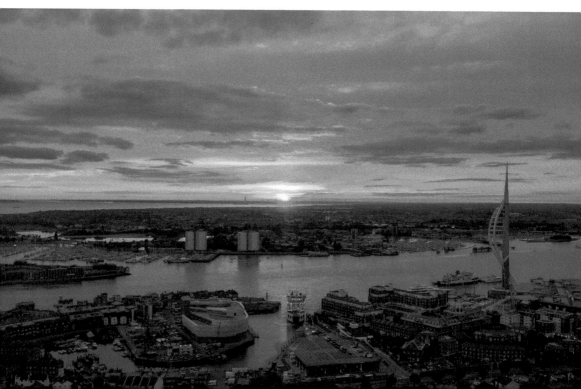

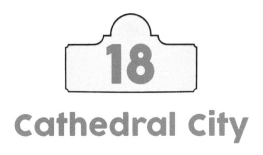

Cathedral City

The Roman Catholics were the first to have a cathedral in Portsmouth. Land sited next to the town's first public park – originally to be called the People's Park but renamed after the Queen – was secured in 1878, the year Victoria Park opened. The Cathedral of St John the Evangelist was built in three stages and completed in 1906.

The Portsmouth Anglican Cathedral is the oldest surviving building in the city. Parts of it were described by Pevsner as 'of the finest architectural quality, in the mainstream of South English tradition', but it was not built as a cathedral.

The Norman Lord Jean de Gisors, a wealthy merchant and shipping magnate who traded largely in hides, saw the potential of the area at the mouth of the harbour for cross-channel trading, as opposed to the top of the harbour at

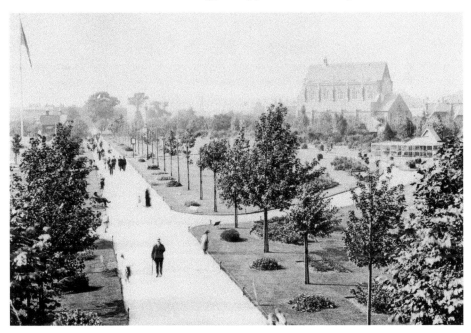

View of Victoria Park and the first stage of the building of St John's Catholic Cathedral in the 1880s.

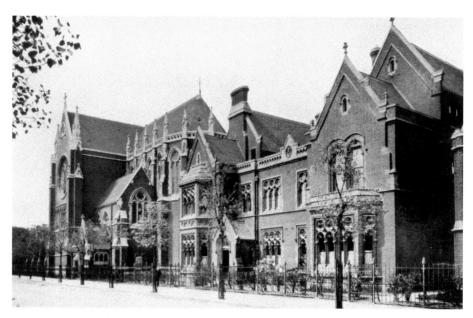

St John's Cathedral in the 1900s.

Portchester, which was silting up and in decline. He bought the Manor of Bocheland (Buckland), the southern part of which was to become Portsmouth. In around 1180 he gave over an acre of land and founded a small chapel which was dedicated to the recently martyred St Thomas à Becket. The chancel and transepts survive from this period.

St Thomas's chapel became the parish church of the growing seaport in 1320. The tower and nave were badly damaged during the Civil War by Parliament forces firing cannon across the harbour from Gosport, reputedly prompting a resentment and rivalry that continues to this day. The church was patched up but, by the 1660s, was in danger of collapsing in on the congregation and so worship took place in the Domus Dei (later the Royal Garrison Church). Rebuilding took place between 1683 and 1693 and extensions were made. In 1702, a wooden cupola was built on the tower and eight new bells cast. A 6-foot-long golden barque of gilded copper serving as a weathervane was added in 1710.

Pew rents helped pay for the upkeep and costs and ensured that the richest Christians got the best seats, the humble poor at the back straining to hear that it was they who would inherit the earth. The north transept gallery was erected in 1750. Ironically called the 'Best Gallery', it was described as 'not so handsome' and was used to accommodate children from the workhouse in Warblington Street. These children had 'PP' marked in large letters on their right sleeve to identify them as 'Portsmouth Pauper' both to others and as a reminder to themselves.

Various alterations were made during the eighteenth and nineteenth centuries and in 1902, complaints of 'foul emanations' led to closure for two years while the foundations were cleared and the church made sanitary and safe. During the clearance, the vicar, Revd Daniel C. Darnell, rolled up his sleeves to help out but contracted typhoid from which he died.

While most pew rents across the country had been abolished by the turn of the century, St Thomas's persisted in this 'ticketing', though both vicars after the First World War (Revds William H. David and E. Neville Lovett) were opposed to the practice. It was argued in vestry meetings that there were 'strong reasons' why it should continue, but the practice was eventually abolished when a new Anglican diocese was formed in 1927 and St Thomas's became a cathedral. Work was started in 1935 to enlarge the church into a small cathedral but was suspended due to the war and the western part of the nave was blocked off, temporarily, with a plain brick wall. The extension, which included a fourth bay of the nave and towers, was eventually built in 1990–91 and consecrated in the presence of the Queen Mother. The cathedral's summoning peal of bells, familiar to residents three centuries ago, was augmented by two additional pairs in 1957 and 2009, and is a timeless and reassuring celebration of continuity, life and of living in Old Portsmouth.

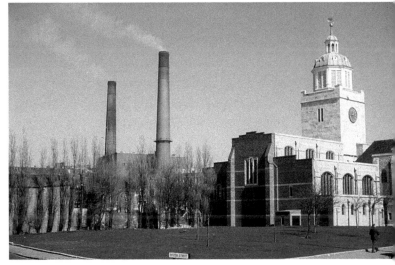

St Thomas's Anglican Cathedral in the 1960s.

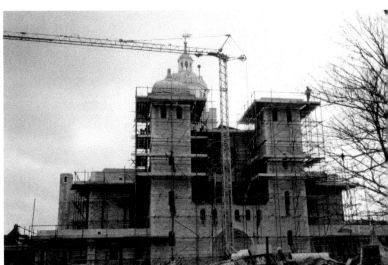

Building of the cathedral extension in 1991.

Celebrating the Spirit of Portsmouth

If there is such a thing as a Portsmouth spirit then it is not something that is easily analysed or defined. Generally, the character of island populations is not portrayed in a very positive light. But oddness and insularity have not, by and large, afflicted the people of this proud island city.

The first recorded bridge linking Portsea Island to the mainland is believed to date from the twelfth century, and since then, many bridges and links have developed, to the extent that it is perfectly possible for visitors and even inhabitants to be unaware that they are on an island. The historic Portsmouth/London Road enabled stagecoaches to reach the capital in just nine hours in the eighteenth century. Today the M275 is the principal route for entering and leaving and continues as the A3, largely following the same route as the old road.

The naval and commercial ports have linked Portsmouth to the Empire and the rest of the world for much of its history. Its role as a naval and garrison town has also brought a historically transient military population, with a large part of local employment and the local economy dependent on servicing

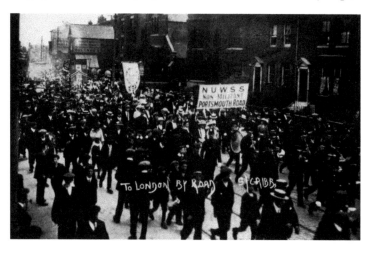

Local women's march to London to fight for the right to vote, 1913. They are seen here passing Charles Dickens' birthplace in Commercial Road. They were pelted with fruit and insults en route.

it. The number of local people who served in, or had members of the family join, the armed services has helped ensure a tradition of patriotism, which together with an island-city pride feeds into any notion of a Pompey spirit or character. In more recent years the university has attracted students from all over the world, helping to create and maintain a vibrant and cosmopolitan island city.

Portsmouth has provided a welcome refuge and a permanent home for many people fleeing persecution and war for centuries, and that tradition continues to this day. Perhaps the most prominent diaspora, so far, is that of the Eastern European Jews. The struggle for civil rights for Jews was a regular issue at Portsmouth council meetings in the nineteenth century. The town council presented a petition to the House of Commons on five occasions in the mid-nineteenth century urging the end of many ways Jews were legally discriminated against. Emanuel Emanuel became the first Jewish town councillor in 1844 and was elected Portsmouth's first Jewish mayor in 1867. Emanuel was instrumental in opening up the town to the railway and spurring and shaping the development of Portsmouth and Southsea.

By 1890, full male emancipation for Jews was achieved but anti-Semitism remained rife, sustained in part by fears prompted by the mass emigration of Jewish refugees escaping persecution in Tsarist Russia. Apart from London, Portsmouth was reported to have the largest Jewish population in the country. This increased during the 1930s at the time of the rise of fascism in Europe. Meanwhile, in Southsea, regular open-air meetings of the British Union of Fascists took place on the seafront and blackshirt rallies were held in the town, led by their leader, Sir Oswald Mosley. While fascism undoubtedly had a few supporters in the city, Mosley and his blackshirts were heckled, barracked and made to feel very unwelcome by Portsmouth's trade unionists and Labour supporters on more than one occasion.

Historically and proudly, Portsmouth people have not been reticent in displaying anti-authoritarian spirit whenever there have been palpable injustices, threat to livelihoods or important principles at stake. Those fights have ranged from life or death issues to the 2015 campaign to prevent the Spinnaker Tower being painted red, the colour of Southampton football team's shirts. Dockyard workers have defended their jobs and livelihoods, council tenants have conducted rent strikes, students have fought causes, and anti-war demonstrations have filled the Town Hall Square. The following selected examples of collective action by Portsmouth people, over half a millennium, tell of struggle, defiance and a Pompey spirit that is better illustrated than described.

In 1628 the deeply unpopular Duke of Buckingham was assassinated in the Greyhound pub in the High Street, now known as Buckingham House. The Duke was an intimate favourite of King James and was widely viewed as lacking in competence. John Felton, the murderer, was tried and hanged at Tyburn and his body sent to be displayed on Southsea Common. Gibbeting, or 'hanging in chains', was intended to disgrace the subject and deter others, but, for many people in Portsmouth, Felton's Gibbet became an object of veneration.

What is believed to have been the first co-operative society in Britain was set up in Portsmouth in 1796 by dockyard workers who were fed up with being ripped off by local tradesmen. The aim of the early co-operators was to offer an alternative by organising and controlling the production and distribution of goods and services under a system operated by and for the people. The Portsea Island co-operative was set up by a handful of volunteers in a rented corner shop in Charles Street in 1873.

In 1817 – two years before the Peterloo massacre – a great Reform meeting was held on Portsdown Hill at which a petition to Parliament was adopted, pleading for universal suffrage (which meant men over twenty-one at that time) and annual elections. Between 20,000 and 50,000 people (including William Cobbett) came from miles around to protest despite magistrates having posted warnings on toll gates and distributing handbills threatening all who valued their safety to keep away. The Hampshire Yeomanry Cavalry was called out in force, the garrison guns were loaded and the town placed under virtual siege. In the event, it was reported that 'no animosity, no riot disturbed the proceedings of the day' and the petition was presented to Parliament. The town, and country, had to wait some fifteen years before the electoral franchise was extended, due to strong opposition from the Tories. The Reform Act of 1832 extended the vote to the middle classes, increasing the electorate to just one in seven males.

In 1826, a 'numerous and respectable meeting of the inhabitants of the Borough of Portsmouth' took place at the Beneficial Society's Hall in Kent Street, Portsea. The meeting, with Mayor David Spice in the chair, resolved to petition the Lords and Commons with an issue that troubled many people across the country. 'Slavery,' the meeting decided, 'under any form or circumstance, however mild or plausible, is contrary to the dictates of justice, as well as repugnant to sound and enlightened policy and that the principles and benign spirit of Christianity are equally opposed to its inhumanity'. Though slave trading had been abolished in 1807, 'a state of the most rigorous and cruel slavery' continued in the British colonies in the West Indies. The condition of the slave population, the meeting heard, 'remains as wretched and merciless as ever'.

Chartist meetings at Portsmouth were reported to be well attended, with people of all classes turning up to hear the arguments for democracy. The vast majority of people did not have the right to vote and the Chartist speakers put the case for greater enfranchisement intelligently and with passion. In April 1839, the Beneficial Society allowed their building in Kent Street to be used for three meetings by Henry Vincent. He was so erudite and achingly reasonable that the editor of the *Portsmouth Times* refused to believe he was a Chartist. The audience included the Mayor, the Lieutenant Governor, the Port Admiral and the Vicar of Portsmouth. Vincent received 'cordial cheers' and there was no sign of the 'seditious', 'treasonable', 'detestable', and 'un-English' revolutionary that the editor of the *Hampshire Advertiser*, who wasn't there, described. He roundly criticised the Beneficial Society for allowing a Chartist to speak there. Less than a year later, three prominent, but possibly less measured Chartists, were sentenced to be hanged, drawn and quartered. The sentence was commuted to penal transportation for life and the prisoners arrived at Portsmouth for incarceration in the prison ship *York* in Portsmouth Harbour, to await transportation to Australia.

Women who sold sex had a tradition of protest in defence of their livelihoods in Portsmouth. In 1861, the *Hampshire Telegraph* headline 'A Parade of Vice' told how women marched through the streets arm in arm following a campaign against their profession by police and magistrates. Six years later, as a result of this 'Crusade Against Vice', it was reported that 300–400 women marched noisily through the Prospect Row area. It took three or four policemen to arrest a woman who they claimed was the ringleader, Susannah Clarke, and 'the mob threw mud, stones, potatoes, and other rubbish at the constables'.

Miss Sarah Robinson, a Christian lady, devoted her life to 'combating evil influences' that surrounded soldiers and sailors in garrison and naval towns. In 1874, she converted the Fountain pub in the High Street into a refuge – The Soldiers' Institute – providing men with somewhere to stay removed from the temptations of prostitutes, alcohol and gambling. Raising money from influential Christian supporters, more 'notorious houses' were bought up, including the Sailors' Welcome near the Dockyard gate which she filled with bibles and 220 beds. Local working women accused Miss Robinson of 'taking the bread out of other people's mouths'. On 5 November 1877, on Southsea Common, Guy Fawkes was reprieved and an effigy of Miss Robinson was burned.

In 1874, the Mayor read the Riot Act and sent troops armed with live ammunition to disperse 3,000–4,000 people from Southsea Common. They had gathered there in defence of the right of free access to the Common for ordinary people, and for the right of access along Southsea beach. These rights were threatened by the commercial interests of the Pier Company. In a confrontation that lasted four days, staves were issued by the police to their supporters who, with the police, indiscriminately and brutally beat up those who were trying to keep the Common open, as well as bystanders. No shots were fired and the defenders of the common achieved their aims.

In 1891 a mass campaign was launched to save a young, unmarried domestic servant from being executed after she had been found guilty at Winchester Assizes of murdering her newborn baby at Ventnor. It was a campaign supported by women of all classes in Portsmouth who organised, attended mass public meetings, knocked doors, wrote letters and petitioned. It had not been established in court whether the baby had been stillborn. A petition demanding a reprieve was started at the *Evening News* office in Arundel Street and within seventeen days over 52,000 people from the town had visited and signed, an estimated one-third of the population. The treatment of the condemned woman, Fanny Gane, was contrasted with that of a well-to-do woman who kept one of her children isolated and tied up in a dark cupboard where she died. The mother received a prison sentence of twelve months; Fanny Gane was condemned to be hanged.

The sense of injustice gripped the town and in particular women, many of whom were doggedly active in building support. A half-a-mile-long petition was delivered to the Home Secretary who, three days later, granted a reprieve but imposed a sentence of life imprisonment. A further petition was organised by the women to quash that sentence, arguing that her only crime was 'concealment of birth'. After nearly five further years of tireless campaigning, Fanny Gane was released.

In 1908 a mass meeting demanding the vote for women was held in the Town Hall, described as one of the largest political events ever held there. The following year, Christabel Pankhurst spoke and, again, the Town Hall was packed. Afterwards, from the Town Hall steps, she addressed another 2,000–3,000 people. In 1913 a suffragist march from Portsmouth to London set off from the Town Hall Square. Described as a pilgrimage, all sympathisers with the women's movement were invited. When they reached Petersfield they were booed, heckled, hustled and their wagon turned over.

Two years after the First World War, a mass demonstration of demobilised servicemen and veterans took place on Southsea Common against government inaction over unemployment, lack of affordable housing, disability pensions and pensions. The Prime Minister's promise of 'a land fit for heroes' was an 'insult to all who have served the country' and it was claimed that the government had been corrupted by vested interests. They demanded that public works be launched to create useful jobs.

In 1926, a march in support of the General Strike set off from the Trades Hall in Fratton Road to Southsea Common where there was a mass meeting of up to 4,000 people. The march was headed by a man with a Davy lamp and a pit pony. Coal miners' wages had been cut by up to 25 per cent and their working hours extended by the coal owners who were anxious to maintain their profits. Other trade unions wanted to help defend their fellow workers and local tramway workers, railwaymen, engineers, firemen, woodworkers and bricklayers were amongst those taking part in the march. There was reported to be 'one red flag, silk and embroidered and carried by a small girl', but the demonstration was 'conducted in an orderly fashion'. A total of 150 local tramway workers lost their jobs when the council refused to take them back after the strike.

In recent years there have been demonstrations against the government's cuts to vital public services and austerity policies that have made the poor poorer, mass rallies about inaction over global warming and demonstrations asserting that Black Lives Matter.

The belief that we never appreciate things until they have gone does not entirely hold water. Throughout its history, large numbers of Portsmuthians have fought to improve the city and their lives, and increasingly to defend things that they value and to assert what they believe is right and just. At a time when nothing can be taken for granted and beloved institutions, rights and services are under ideological and economic threat from central government and big business, many people in the city are beginning to protest. Pride and principles, it seems, together with an undying passion and optimism so evident on match days at Fratton Park, are at the heart of any notion of a Portsmouth spirit. May Pompey, forever, play up!

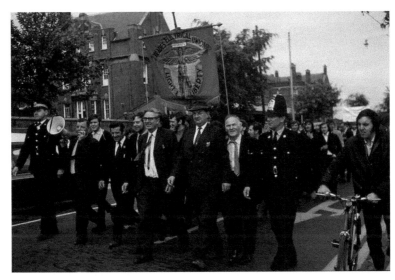

Dockyard walk-out, 1972.

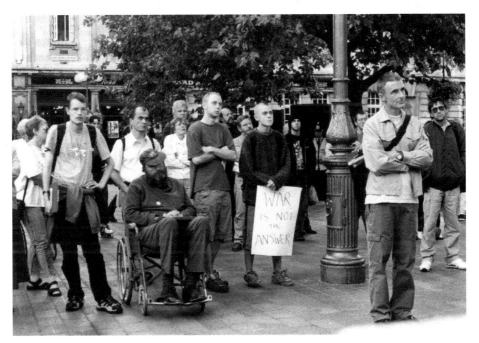

Demonstration against the war in Afghanistan, Guildhall Square, 2001.

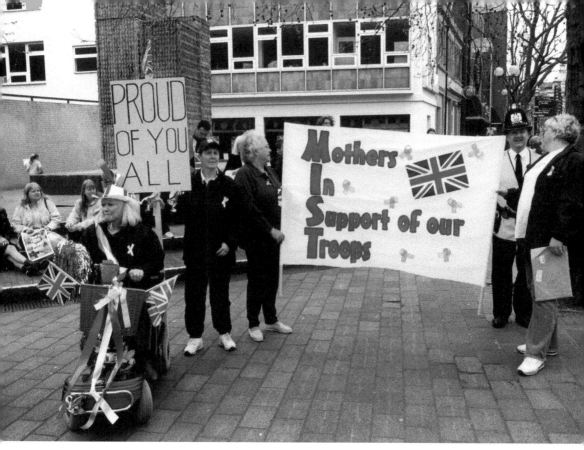

'Support our Troops' demonstration, Guildhall Square, 2003.

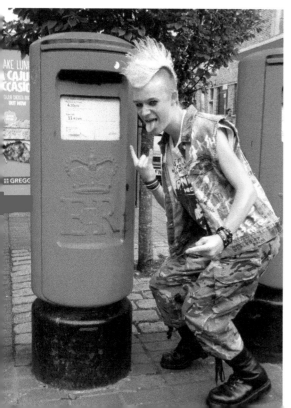

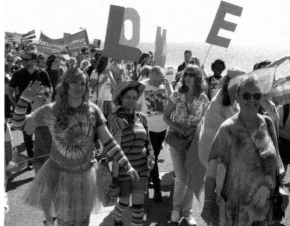

Above: Pride on the prom, 2019.

Left: Punk in Palmerston Road, 2019.

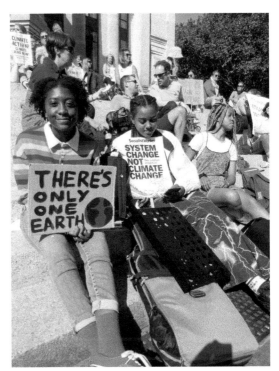

Right: Protest against government inaction over climate change, Guildhall Square, 2019.

Below: Sandra (aka Nan) of Somerstown by artist Karl Rudziak, 2018.

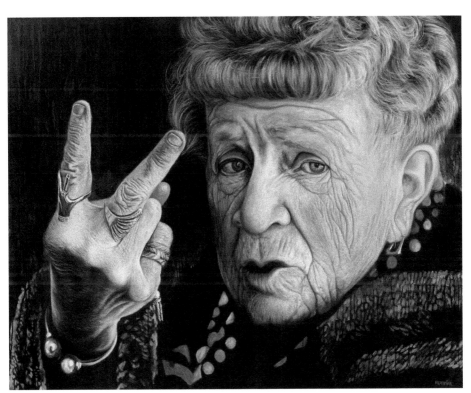

Selected References

PEN/PT: Portsmouth Evening News/Times. HT/HA: Hampshire Telegraph/
Advertiser PCR: Corporation Records. PP: Portsmouth Paper.

Queen: Penny Illustrated 18/7/1903, PEN 11/2/01, 7/1937, 15/2/1955, 21/2/1955, Destruction & Reconstruction 1939-74 (PP no 66) John Stedman, The Buildings of Hampshire & IOW Pevsner and Lloyd (1967),Town Centre Report 1965. **Guildhall:** HA 26 Jul 1899, PCR, Bystander 15 3 1905, HT 21 Jul, 22 Sep 1888, HA 26 Jul 1899, HT 13 Feb 1920, PEN 17 1 41, HT 12 6 1959. **News:** Supplement 22 4 1977. **Dickens**: Portsmouth Corporation Records (PCR), The Guardian 19 Aug 2011. HT 7 Oct 1871, 14 Oct 1871,11 July 1891, 24 Dec 1892, IOW Obs 11 July 1891, The Portmuthian 1883, The Times 6 July 1908, 18 Feb 1997, 25 Feb 1997, 26 Feb 1997. **Mudlarks:** HT 16 7 1954, 10 11 1900, 29 5 1931. **Market:** Notes on the Topography of Portsmouth by A. Howell (1913), Portsmouth not so old, R. Esmond (1961) PEN 7 12 1878, 13 12 1878, 14 12 1878, 13 9 1892, 13 10 1894, 3 10 1932, 4 10 1922, 10 10 1922, 18 10 1922, 23 5 1925, 9 10 1925, 7 12 1932, 22 2 1935, 9 5 1949, 27 6 1949, 14 12 1949, 19 12 1952, 23 2 1955. **Canoe Lake:** PCR, Portsmouth Ward Lock 1902, 1929 guide book, Notes on Southsea F Davidson c 1930, HA 11 7 1914, 13 6 1922, 23 8 1946, 9 10 1959, PEN 22 8 1904, 31 1 35, 24 7 1949, 8 8 1951, 11 3 1953, 28 5 1953. **Spice:** PCR, Topography of Portsmouth A Howell (1913), PEN 12 12 1901, 27 11 1930, 23 2 1934, 21 3 1952, HT 12 5 1922. **Dockyard:** Portsmouth in Defence of the Realm J.Sadden (2001). **Education:** PGS: Opus 9 Winter 2013, The Portsmouth Beneficial School 1755-39 by L Gatt, (PP 46). Reminiscences of Old Portsmouth F J Proctor c1915 PP 77 Portsmouth's Schools 1750-1975 by Peter Galliver. **Common:** HC 27 1 1817, HC 3 9 1821, HT 24 4 1847, HT 8 4 1848, PEN 31 3 1892, PEN 24 4 1894, PEN 24 2 24, PEN 15 10 24, PEN 20 4 27, PEN 17 2 1939, PEN 22 7 1939, The Way about Hampshire & IOW W A Bettesworth (1896), An Earthly Fairyland (Rock Gardens) J Baynes (2013), Portsmouth in Defence of the Realm J.Sadden (2001), Growth of Southsea PP16 Ray Riley (1972) **Pier:** PCR, Mick Cooper, HT 10 11 1877, 8 2 1878, 5 6 1878, 2 4 1881, 20 7 1904, 27 1 1906, 17 3 1906, PEN 26 7 1879, The Stage 27 7 1974. Guide books. **Pompey:** PFC Official Centenary (1998), PEN 26 2 1949, 28 2 1949. **Cathedrals:** Portsmouth Parish Church, Lilley and Everitt (1921), Pevsner. **Spirit:** Portsdown: Manchester Post 12 2 1817 Chartists HA 6 4 1839, 13 4 1839, Brighton Patriot 16 4 1839, Hereford Times 22 2 1840 Fanny Gane PEN 6 1 1892, 12 1 1892, HT 8 1 1896, Women on common/ Robinson HT 20 11 1931, HT 9 2 1861, HT 16 2 1861, Norwich Mercury 11 5 1887, HT 14 9 1867 . Battle of Southsea HT 19 8 1874 PP34 J.Field (1981), Votes for Women PP39 S.Peacock (1983) General Strike PT 7 5 1926, 14 5 1926.